CALLED

By Robert William Cobb

Copyright © 2011 by Robert William Cobb

Called
by Robert William Cobb

Printed in the United States of America

ISBN 9781612158334

All rights reserved solely by the author. The author guarantees all contents are original and do not infringe upon the legal rights of any other person or work. No part of this book may be reproduced in any form without the permission of the author. The views expressed in this book are not necessarily those of the publisher.

Unless otherwise indicated, Bible quotations are taken from The King James Version. Copyright © 1998-2011 by Olive Tree Software; and The NIV. Copyright © 2009 by Tecarta, Inc.

www.xulonpress.com

DEDICATION

First, I would like to thank God for calling me from my mother's womb. Second my mother, Wilda Jane Cobb, who took me to church and prayed for me. Third, every believer who helped me to find my way through the doubt and unbelief. Fourth, my wife, Sarah Cobb, who encouraged me while writing this book. Finally, everyone who is in the fight against the evil one: Those who have been called, and those who are about to be called.

About the cover

You are called to Greatness.

What's holding you back?

Job 39:19-25 (NIV)

"Do you give the horse his strength or clothe his neck with a flowing mane? [20] Do you make him leap like a locust, striking terror with his proud snorting? [21] He paws fiercely, rejoicing in his strength, and charges into the fray. [22] He laughs at fear, afraid of nothing; he does not shy away from the sword. [23] The quiver rattles against his side, along with the flashing spear and lance. [24] In frenzied excitement he eats up the ground; he cannot stand still when the trumpet sounds. [25] At the blast of the trumpet he snorts, `Aha!' He catches the scent of battle from afar, the shout of commanders and the battle cry.

Do you hear the battle cry? Do you hear God's call to arms? If you do, get up and fight. Don't let anything hold you back.

Matthew 11:12

12 And from the days of John the Baptist until now the kingdom of heaven suffereth violence, and the violent take it by force.

About the book

Events that took place in Robert's (R. Bob's) testimony happened between the dates (1994-2002). The book consists of an introduction, a testimony, and a conclusion.

The testimony is divided into eight chapters and contains teaching on the following subjects:

1. Who is the real God?
2. Falling away
3. Witnessing
4. Evangelism
5. Seeing the invisible
6. Discipleship
7. Church relationships
8. Home cell groups

The conclusion contains teaching on the following subjects:

1. Good advice for every believer
2. Overcoming adversity by getting up
3. Prayer and praise
4. Called 21 day prayer workout

After hearing the call of God, Robert (R. Bob) gave up his career, retirement, possessions, family, and friends and went. His testimony and teachings are an inspiration to those who don't know what God has called them to do, have heard God's call but have failed to respond, or have responded to God's call and need encouragement to stay the course.

• note
This book is written as if the reader is in a home cell group or church meeting listening to Robert tell his testimony.

TABLE OF CONTENTS

Page#

About the cover vii
About the book ix
Introduction xiii
Chapter 1 17
Chapter 2 30
Chapter 3 39
Chapter 4 48
Chapter 5 56
Chapter 6 69
Chapter 7 76
Chapter 8 88
Conclusion 93
Prayer notes 123
Called Workout 137
Contact Information 150

Introduction

The Impossible is believable when you spend time with God. So don't use the word impossible as a reason not to try. We can always find a reason not to do something when we don't want to do it.

What is God telling you to do today? Do you hear His call? We are all called to do something, and we need to be obedient to that call.

We are part of a team and a team is only as strong as it's weakest member. If we are all operating in Christ's strength, than we are unbeatable.

When you don't hear or act on the calling that God has placed on you, then there is something that is not being accomplished. It doesn't matter if you are unaware of the danger that you are causing yourself and others. The adversary is taking advantage of your inaction to the call upon your life.

As for my life, God's call came with a set of instructions that were hard to follow without His help and encouragement. First, I had to quit my job. Second, I had to leave my family and friends. Third, I had to go to Bible college in order to connect with God's next step. Finally, I had to give up everything that I owned. Does that sound easy to you?

The result of my obedience is the testimony you are about to read. The amazing thing about my testimony is that you see God's hand at work even when I made mistakes. Also, you can see that someone doesn't have to be perfect in order for God to use them.

1 Samuel 15:22 (NIV)
But Samuel replied: "Does the Lord delight in burnt offerings and sacrifices as much as in obeying the voice of the Lord? To obey is better than sacrifice, and to heed is better than the fat of rams.

God doesn't want us to do religious actions to make us look and feel clean. He wants us to hear His voice and respond in obedience. Even when religious leaders do not agree with your actions.
If you look at the ministry of Jesus, you see someone standing against the religious leaders of His time. So, understand that it is more important to hear God's voice and respond in obedience than dotting the "i" s and crossing the "t"s of your religious thinking.

Hebrews 3:15-16 (NIV)
As has just been said: "Today, if you hear his voice, do not harden your hearts as you did in the rebellion." [16] Who were they who heard and rebelled? Were they not all those Moses led out of Egypt?"

When you hear God's call on your life, do not fall into doubt and unbelief. Believe what God is telling you, and look for help from those brothers and sisters who will love and encourage you in Christ. If you can't find any, God has given you a comforter to love, encourage and direct you in His calling for your life.

Let me encourage you now. Whatever God has told you to do, do it.

Matthew 11:12
12 And from the days of John the Baptist until now the kingdom of heaven suffereth violence, and the violent take it by force.

God has called you to fight. DO It!

Romans 3:3-4
3 For what if some did not believe? shall their unbelief make the faith of God without effect? 4 God forbid: yea, let God be true, but every man a liar; as it is written, That thou mightest be justified in thy sayings, and mightest overcome when thou art judged.

God has called you to believe Him – not men. DO IT!

Romans 8:27-31
27 And he that searcheth the hearts knoweth what[is] the mind of the Spirit, because he maketh intercession for the saints according to[the will of] God. 28 And we know that all things work together for good to them that love God, to them who are the called according to[his] purpose. 29 For whom he did foreknow, he also did predestinate[to be] conformed to the image of his Son, that he might be the firstborn among many brethren. 30 Moreover whom he did predestinate, them he also called: and whom he called, them he also justified: and whom he justified, them he also glorified. 31 What shall we then say to these things? If God[be] for us, who[can be] against us?

God is for those He has called. DO IT!

Chapter 1

I was always one who liked to joke around and be the class clown. This got me some favor when I was younger, but it didn't help me pay the bills in my life. Although I still like to be humorous, not everybody gets me.

I was the life of the party. I had the best friends money could buy, but when I stopped buying, my friends stopped coming around. They would laugh at my jokes when I was paying the price, but after I stopped paying the price, I became the joke.

This is where my testimony begins. It begins with a lost lifestyle. I knew it was time to stop drinking. I knew that the party was over, and that major changes were needed in my life. So, I went to rehab for one month seeking new answers. However, the answers were not in rehab or any twelve step program. They were revealed to me through a process of seeking to find the truth and learning how to ask the right questions.

I always believed there was a power greater than myself, and for most of my adult life I believed that greater power was Jesus. However, I started to question that assumption, and I wanted to know who God really was. This question, "Who is the real God?" is a question men and women ask themselves every day, but it's not a new question.

Who is the real God?
1 Kings 18:20-39
20 So Ahab sent for all the children of Israel, and gathered the prophets together on Mount Carmel. 21 And Elijah came to all the people, and said, "How long will you falter between two opinions? If the LORD is God, follow Him; but if Baal, follow him." But the people answered him not a word. 22 Then Elijah said to the people, "I alone am left a prophet of the LORD; but Baal's prophets are four hundred and fifty men. 23 Therefore let them give us two bulls; and let them choose one bull for themselves, cut it in pieces, and lay it on the wood, but put no fire under it; and I will prepare the other bull, and lay it on the wood, but put no fire under it. 24 Then you call on the name of your gods, and I will call on the name of the LORD; and the God who answers by fire, He is God."
So all the people answered and said, "It is well spoken."
25 Now Elijah said to the prophets of Baal, "Choose one bull for yourselves and prepare it first, for you are many; and call on the name of your god, but put no fire under it."
26 So they took the bull which was given them, and they prepared it, and called on the name of Baal from morning even till noon, saying, "O Baal, hear us!" But there was no voice; no one answered. Then they leaped about the altar which they had made.
27 And so it was, at noon, that Elijah mocked them and said, "Cry aloud, for he is a god; either he is meditating, or he is busy, or he is on a journey, or perhaps he is sleeping and must be awakened." 28 So they cried aloud, and cut themselves, as was their custom,

with knives and lances, until the blood gushed out on them. 29 And when midday was past, they prophesied until the time of the offering of the evening sacrifice. But there was no voice; no one answered, no one paid attention. 30 Then Elijah said to all the people, "Come near to me." So all the people came near to him. And he repaired the altar of the LORD that was broken down. 31 And Elijah took twelve stones, according to the number of the tribes of the sons of Jacob, to whom the word of the LORD had come, saying, "Israel shall be your name."[b] 32 Then with the stones he built an altar in the name of the LORD; and he made a trench around the altar large enough to hold two seahs of seed. 33 And he put the wood in order, cut the bull in pieces, and laid it on the wood, and said, "Fill four waterpots with water, and pour it on the burnt sacrifice and on the wood." 34 Then he said, "Do it a second time," and they did it a second time; and he said, "Do it a third time," and they did it a third time. 35 So the water ran all around the altar; and he also filled the trench with water.
36 And it came to pass, at the time of the offering of the evening sacrifice, that Elijah the prophet came near and said, "LORD God of Abraham, Isaac, and Israel, let it be known this day that You are God in Israel and I am Your servant, and that I have done all these things at Your word. 37 Hear me, O LORD, hear me, that this people may know that You are the LORD God, and that You have turned their hearts back to You again."
38 Then the fire of the LORD fell and consumed the burnt sacrifice, and the wood and the stones and the dust, and it licked up the water that was in the trench. 39 Now when all the people saw it, they fell on their faces; and they said, "The LORD, He is God! The LORD, He is God!"

Lord Jesus is the real God!
(Matthew 16:16)

Unfortunately, I didn't know that then. I could have studied this Bible passage anytime growing up, since I was baptized at age 12, but I chose not to learn it. However, I heard about Elijah in Sunday school.

Romans 15:4
For everything that was written in the past were written to teach us, so that through the endurance taught in the Scriptures and the encouragement they provide we might have hope.

Everything that was written in the scriptures was written to teach us. Therefore, you do not have to learn from your life experiences, also known as the school of hard knocks. Unfortunately for me, I was unaware and/or lacked understanding of these scriptures. So, I had to learn my lessons the hard way.

After coming out of rehab, I started to go to AA meetings, and I focused on working the twelve step program that was a big part of my recovery. During this process, I started asking questions about my faith:

Did I believe in Jesus because I grew up in the church?

Was God found in another faith or belief?

Did God Exist?

Who is the real God?

So, with these questions in mind, I started my search for God.

The Search
The first step for me was meditation. I had an idea how to meditate, and I followed that idea. I would

run 5 to 6 miles a day, and I would meditate as I ran. Sometimes the run was very easy because my mind was somewhere else focused on meditating as I ran.

I begin to have out of body experiences. I could see myself running, and I could soar like a bird and watch myself run from great heights. Then I would come back to my body and resume the run.

It was during one of these runs that something jumped on my back. I perceived that the spirit was an evil one, and I wrestled with it for a while before I threw it off.

At this point, my meditation started to change direction. I began to read books on meditation, and I learned about gateways called shock-eras that I could open by using meditation.

After opening these gateways, I moved toward the Native American belief of shamanism. I had a fondness for the North American Indian culture and that attracted me to read and study books concerning their ideology.

From there, it didn't take me long before I was performing rituals in that belief and developing my spiritual power. My first spirit guide was a gray wolf. He told me that he was one of my ancestors from my mom's side of the family. This spirit stated that he was from the Blackfoot Indian tribe and he was a medicine man. He started to guide me in what I had to do to become a medicine man.

The next thing I knew I was preparing for a vision quest. You may wonder what a vision quest is. It's a Native American Indian rite of passage. When it was time for a child to take his or her place with the adults, he or she would go into the wilderness for several days. This included fasting and meditating for the purpose of obtaining a direction for one's life. Also, a guardian animal may help in ones vision.

I undertook this vision quest at the direction of my spirit guide. On my third day of fasting, while I was in the woods, I felt and heard heavy breathing behind my neck. I did not open my eyes or dared to leave the circle of protection that I had prepared.

After the fear passed away for several minutes, I opened my eyes. I saw a beautiful buck deer. He looked at me, and I looked at him. He was not afraid of me, and I was not afraid of him. We existed together in the calm for a length of time before the buck finally went his way.

When I finished my vision quest, I started home. I saw two more deer along the way and they were not afraid of me, and I didn't fear them. It was amazing to see wildlife so close without any fear or danger in the situation. Also, later that day I saw a fawn prancing around as if to dance before me.

At this stage, I began to meet with a local Native American shaman. He had a small Indian crafts shop in Manistee, Michigan. He informed me about Indian ways, and I started to go to Native American events.

I would like to take a break from my testimony at this point to explain something I learned in this process of searching:

Romans 1:18-25
18 For the wrath of God is revealed from heaven against all ungodliness and unrighteousness of men, who hold the truth in unrighteousness;
19 Because that which may be known of God is manifest in them; for God hath shewed it unto them.
20 For the invisible things of him from the creation of the world are clearly seen, being understood by the things that are made, even his eternal power and Godhead; so that they are without excuse:

21 Because that, when they knew God, they glorified him not as God, neither were thankful; but became vain in their imaginations, and their foolish heart was darkened.
22 Professing themselves to be wise, they became fools,
23 And changed the glory of the uncorruptible God into an image made like to corruptible man, and to birds, and fourfooted beasts, and creeping things.
24 Wherefore God also gave them up to uncleanness through the lusts of their own hearts, to dishonour their own bodies between themselves:
25 Who changed the truth of God into a lie, and worshipped and served the creature more than the Creator, who is blessed for ever. Amen.

There is a procedure for falling away from God. Romans 1:21 shows you that procedure. First, you must esteem God more valuable than anything else in your life.

Daniel 11:36-37
36 And the king shall do according to his will; and he shall exalt himself, and magnify himself above every god, and shall speak marvellous things against the God of gods, and shall prosper till the indignation be accomplished: for that that is determined shall be done.
37 Neither shall he regard the God of his fathers, nor the desire of women, nor regard any god: for he shall magnify himself above all.

So, the first step to fall away from the knowledge of God in your heart is to esteem self knowledge above the knowledge of God.

I qualified for this step when I even questioned the fact that Jesus was God. Therefore, when I started this question process, I was already on a slippery slope.

Second, they weren't thankful.

Philippians 4:4
Rejoice in the Lord always: and again I say, Rejoice.

This is a command to continually rejoice in the Lord. When you don't, then you are moving even further away from the knowledge of God.
I wasn't rejoicing in the Lord. Instead, I was following human logic. Therefore, I was sliding further away from the truth.

Third, their imaginations became vain.

2 Corinthians 10:3-5
3 For though we walk in the flesh, we do not war after the flesh:
4 (For the weapons of our warfare are not carnal, but mighty through God to the pulling down of strong holds;)
5 Casting down imaginations, and every high thing that exalteth itself against the knowledge of God, and bringing into captivity every thought to the obedience of Christ;

The war is in the mind. The enemy wants you to think about anything except the knowledge of God.
Satan had me chasing a bunny trail, and I was sliding and sliding down that slop. My imagination was vain.

Fourth, their hearts became darkened.

Ephesians 4:18
Having the understanding darkened, being alienated from the life of God through the ignorance that is in them, because of the blindness of their heart:

You are totally alienated from the knowledge of God at this step. Whether I made it this far or not, I don't know, but I believe I was somewhere in the neighborhood.

So, falling away is exactly what it is: a process of falling away. I wanted you to see that it is a process, and anyone could be in any stage of the process and have no idea that their falling in the first place.

I had no idea I was running a hundred miles an hour in the wrong direction. I started to do things that I wouldn't have done at the beginning of the process. The devil twisted my direction a little bit and he continued to twist, bit by bit, until I was so twisted that what I considered wrong before seemed approvable and right.

I was practicing witchcraft at this point and casting spells. I could tell you everything about a person even their deepest darkest secrets just by touching their photograph. In spite of all that, I came to believe my spirit guide was not an Indian shaman, wolf or buck, but someone with a greater name. My spirit guide told me his name was, "Jesus".

When I was at my lowest, I went to Texas to meet with a witch that was part of a coven. I knew her boyfriend, and he set up the meeting between us. The purpose of the meeting was to set up a band. I arrived in Texas with a warning from my spirit guide "Jesus".

He said, "Beware of the red headed man." I heard this warning over and over again.

However, when the woman picked me up, I saw no red headed man. She took me to several places where witches hung out, and she talk to me about starting a band.

It wasn't until we arrived at her place that I saw the red headed man. He came from nowhere. It is possible that he was in the back of the van the whole time. He looked very angry, but I kept my distance since I had been warned about him already.

The woman calmed him down and he left. She informed me that he was part of her coven. She then told me that Jesus was an inappropriate spirit guide, and she directed me in a meditation to change my spirit guide.

Then we talk more about the band, and she took me back to my motel room and dropped me off.

I left Texas prepared to start this band with this witch coven. However, shortly after I returned home, the person that introduced me to the woman called me. As soon as I answered the phone, I could see shadow figures moving around the room, and I could hear chanting. He said," they are after me. I broke up with her, and her coven is after me." I advised him to get baptized immediately, and I continued using magic to fight magic.

I'm not kidding you! I told him to get baptized, and I continued to do magic. Can you see the inner conflict I was dealing with? On one hand, from somewhere inside of me, I knew to tell this man to go to a church and get baptized, but on the other hand, I was still operating in witchcraft. God was present in my situation here, and I didn't even realize it at the time.

The man that introduced me to the women who was a witch called me back. He told me that he went to the local church and was baptized. He had experienced no problems since then. However, I was still fighting off these shadow figures with magic spells and burning sage brush.

After two weeks of dealing with these shadow figures, I received relief from my situation. I went to work, and I saw a Bible scripture lying on the secretary's desk. I read the scripture (Genesis 3:5) and it lit up my soul. I had a God encounter, and for the first time in my life I knew that the God of the bible was real, and that I was in the wrong thing.

I called everyone that I knew and told them about what I experienced and that the lord Jesus is God. My Soul was on fire for the things of God. I joined the local church and was baptized. I read the whole Bible several times.

Now, look at Genesis 3:5:
For God doth know that in the day ye eat thereof, then your eyes shall be opened, and ye shall be as gods, knowing good and evil.

It's funny! That the scripture that talks about how man became spiritually blind became light to me and gave me the spiritual understanding I needed to overcome my ignorance in my situation.

God is amazing, and He works in amazing ways. Amen!

Behind the scenes
there were many believers praying for me and witnessing to me. I never felt threatened by them. I was searching, and I welcomed anyone who wanted to talk about their belief in God.

I worked at a corrections camp as an officer. Many inmates would talk to me about Jesus, as well as various other beliefs. Ralf was one of those inmates who would talk to me about his relationship with Jesus. Also, there was an Officer named Jerry who spent time with me outside the correction camp.

It was during this time, I was inspired by the Holy Spirit to write the parable of the Ignorant Child.

The Parable of the Ignorant Child

There was a certain child that thought he knew his father. He knew his father from what he had seen and heard from home. He knew his father from what others had told him about his father. Because he was young and foolish, he let others give him a false opinion of his father; that opinion stayed with the child a long time.

The child was playing in his father's house when one day he found a book. The book was his father's diary. The child thought it would be wrong to read the book, so he did not read it.

Sometime after that, the child was talking with some friends; they said something about his father that didn't seem right. The child tried to defend his father, but his friends seem to know his father better than him, so he started to think that maybe his father wasn't who he thought he was.

The child remembered where he had found his father's diary, and he decided to seek the truth for himself. He opened the book and started to read those things his friends had said about his father were true. Out of grief, he put down the book and moved against his father. He began to fellowship with the friends that had told him about his father.

However, after a period of time, the child decided to read the whole diary. The child went back to the hiding

Called

place, picked up the diary, and read it from cover to cover.

His opinions started to change; the child realized that he had judged his father without knowing him. He had let friends and strangers control his thinking. He had let a partial reading of the truth twist what he had seen in his father. The child also discovered that the more he read his father's diary, the more he understood he was loved. Through reading the diary several times, the child knew his father.

Read:
2 Peter 3:16 (NIV)
…His letters contain some things that are hard to understand, which ignorant and unstable people distort, as they do the other Scriptures, to their own destruction.

Please, reread the parable for a deeper understanding.

Chapter 2

1 Peter 2:9
But ye[are] a chosen generation, a royal priesthood, an holy nation, a peculiar people; that ye should shew forth the praises of him who hath called you out of darkness into his marvellous light:

We are called out of darkness into His marvelous light. In his light we see light. The word of God is light, and His children are filled with His light.

1 Thessalonians 5:5
Ye are all the children of light, and the children of the day: we are not of the night, nor of darkness.

There were many believers praying for me and witnessing to me during my search for the true God. I never felt threatened by any of them. I was searching, and I welcomed anyone who wanted to talk to me about their belief in God.

I worked at a corrections camp as an officer. Many inmates would talk to me about Jesus, as well as various other beliefs. Ralf was one of those inmates who would talk to me about his relationship with Jesus.

Also, there was an officer named Jerry who spent time with me outside the correction camp.

Once God's light delivered me from the dark place I was in, these two men became my fathers in Christ. They help me throughout a difficult period in my life.

I would like to say that everything was fine after I was baptized, but it wasn't all a bed of roses. I had subjected myself to some very evil spirits who didn't want to let go of me. Even to this day there is some residual evil that fines cracks in my armor and harasses me continuously. However, the great news is God's grace is sufficient, and I can do all things through Christ who strengthens me.

I was on fire for God. I couldn't get to the mission field fast enough. I witnessed to everybody I met. I would work Jesus into the conversation one way or another. My Co-workers and the inmates at the corrections camp got the best of it.

I would have bible studies with groups of inmates and encourage them to witness to other inmates and staff. Also, the church I was attending conducted church services at the corrections camp every week. So, it was easy to get the materials we needed for witnessing and many people were conquered by God's love.

We would dance and rejoice every time someone received Jesus as their savior. It was all about the fire of revival on all of us. There was no greater joy than to see someone choose to enter the kingdom of God.

I would go to church very excited about fellowshipping and hearing God's word. I was like a kid in a candy store. I could not get enough of God. I became what is known as a "Jesus freak". I ate, breath, and talked about Jesus 24 hours a day/ 7 days a week.

I noticed right away that other brothers and sisters in Christ weren't as excited as I seem to be. I would hear things like, "You need to sit down for two years before you get up and start leading the charge". The thing was I was so on fire for God I could not be quiet. When you have a good thing you have to tell everybody. Even the world knows that.

Ephesians 5:6
Let no man deceive you with vain words: for because of these things cometh the wrath of God upon the children of disobedience.

I kept hearing God in my heart telling me one thing, "Go!" and complacent brothers and sisters in Christ telling me something else. You be the witness. Should I have listened to God or man?

Hebrews 6:17-19
17 Wherein God, willing more abundantly to shew unto the heirs of promise the immutability of his counsel, confirmed it by an oath:
18 That by two immutable things, in which it was impossible for God to lie, we might have a strong consolation, who have fled for refuge to lay hold upon the hope set before us:
19 Which hope we have as an anchor of the soul, both sure and stedfast, and which entereth into that within the veil;

God was and is my soul's anchor, and He does not lie. When I receive a true word from God, I know that I know that I know that I know it's from God.
I'm not saying that's the only way He instructs us, but it is the way that there is no doubt about what He instructed. We are all called to preach the Gospel, and there is no time of service disclaimer on the command,

"Go!". Go means go and preach means preach. It's every believers labor of love.

Mark 16:15
And he said unto them, Go ye into all the world, and preach the gospel to every creature.

1 Corinthians 8:16
For though I preach the gospel, I have nothing to glory of: for necessity is laid upon me; yea, woe is unto me, if I preach not the gospel!

Through my testimony and my child-like faith in the Gospel of Christ, many people received Jesus as their savior. I would tell anybody who would listen about the kingdom of God that existed within me.

Romans 1:16
For I am not ashamed of the gospel, because it is the power of God that brings salvation to everyone who believes:

I believe that we are all called as witnesses for the true witness is the Holy Spirit that dwells within us, and as long as we are willing to listen to Him, and not self, people can share God's free gift regardless of how long you have been a believer. This is because everyone who is saved has and is a witness.

John 15:26-27
26 When the Counselor comes, whom I will send to you from the father, the spirit of truth that goes out from the Father, he will testify about me. 27 And you also must testify, for you have been with me from the beginning.

Now! You and I have not been with Jesus from the beginning, but we have the Counselor and the words written by those who have. Anyone who speaks God's written word to someone is a witness.

Acts 13:5
When they arrived at Salamis, they proclaimed the word of God in the Jewish synagogues. John was with them as their helper.

    I remember my coworker Jerry went with me to pick out a Bible shortly before I was brought back from the brink of destruction. I found a bible I really liked, and we went to the Native American Indian shop. I showed the shaman my new Bible and he didn't seem to be as happy as I was about it.
    I also remember how Jerry didn't judge me in what I said and did but just encouraged me to read the word of God. I read some passages in my Bible when I purchased it, but it didn't mean much to me until that day the word of God was illuminated in my heart.
    In addition, Ralf was feeding me scriptures all the time in a way that I perceived as kind and caring. He was easy to talk to and he never seemed to push any issue too hard or come across as a religious fanatic.
    So, behind the scenes of my revelation of the true God were faithful believers who were helping me find the true God. I'm sure there were many others like my mother and her prayer partners who were waging war on my behalf. I want to take time to thank these people and every other brother and sister who has, is and will be helping others into a firm relationship with Jesus Christ through prayer and witnessing and any other way God leads them.
    I would like to point out:

Several believers prayed.

James 5:16
The effectual fervent prayer of a righteous man availeth much.

Two believers feed me the word.

Romans 10:14-17
14 How then shall they call on him in whom they have not believed? and how shall they believe in him of whom they have not heard? and how shall they hear without a preacher? 15 And how shall they preach, except they be sent? as it is written, How beautiful are the feet of them that preach the gospel of peace, and bring glad tidings of good things! 16 But they have not all obeyed the gospel. For Esaias saith, Lord, who hath believed our report? 17 So then faith[cometh] by hearing, and hearing by the word of God.

I was seeking the truth with my whole heart.

Matthew 7:7-8
7 Ask, and it shall be given you; seek, and ye shall find; knock, and it shall be opened unto you: 8 For every one that asketh receiveth; and he that seeketh findeth; and to him that knocketh it shall be opened.

Paul said it this way:

1 Corinthians 3:5-8
5 Who then is Paul, and who[is] Apollos, but ministers by whom ye believed, even as the Lord gave to every man? 6 I have planted, Apollos watered; but God gave the increase. 7 So then neither is he that planteth any

thing, neither he that watereth; but God that giveth the increase. 8 Now he that planteth and he that watereth are one: and every man shall receive his own reward according to his own labour.

The Holy Spirit through Paul is informing us that we are a team, and when we work together following God's great Devine plan, people are freed from the bondage of this world, and they can enter the kingdom of God.

That's one of the truths I'm trying to show you in my testimony. That when brothers and sisters work together with God, people like myself have received Divine intervention through an illumination of the word, as well as many other ways God has revealed and reveals Himself through the prayers and actions of His saints.

I knew that I knew that I knew that it was time to quit my job. I was attending every Bible study and seminar I could attend and still I wanted to learn more and more.

I saw an advertisement for Marilyn Hickey Bible College. I started to dream about going there. Many people at church and work were trying to talk me out of leaving my job. I had a great job with a good position, but the more I went to church, praised God, and delighted myself in the Lord, the more I wanted to leave my job.

Also, fellow workers started accusing me of all kinds of things such as bringing Bibles into the correctional facility. I had no need to bring Bibles in that way. Because I could bring in as many Bibles as I wanted through my local church who conducted the church services at the corrections camp. However, an accusation this small was only the beginning of slanderous remarks about me at work.

Called

At the same time, there were family members that were opposed to me leaving my career. I heard many good arguments why I shouldn't give up my good paying job. The job had many benefits including retirement and medical insurance. I was just months away from ten years of service which meant I could have received a partial retirement and some medical benefits when I retire. However, I heard God's call and obedience is better than sacrifice.

Confirmation
I was sitting in my home praying one day when the Lord spoke to my heart. He told me to go to the Federal Park by my house and walk north on the beach of Lake Michigan. Also, as I was leaving, I perceived I needed to bring my roller blades and my rollerblading equipment.

When I arrived at the park, I walked north on the beach per instructions. I walked for approximately twenty minutes when I came across a man walking south on the same beach.

I started to tell him about the Lord Jesus Christ and how excited I was to have him in my life. The young man told me he was a first year college student at Arizona State. He continued on his way, and I continued on my way. A few minutes latter I heard a voice from inside me say," Where are you going?"

I said, "I'm walking north on this beach like you told me." I heard, "turn around!" So, I turned around and walked back to my car.

When I arrived at my car, I took out my rollerblades and equipment and went rollerblading in the park.

Even though my rollerblades were expensive and new, I thought I was getting too old to enjoy them. I went back to my car. That's when I saw the first year college student from Arizona State again. I asked him, "Would you like to go skating?" He tried on the rollerblades and he was amazed that they were a perfect fit.

After he went skating, I heard, "Give him the rollerblades"! I started to remember that these rollerblades were the top of the line and very expensive, so I hesitated. Again, I heard," Give him the roller blades". So, I wrote a note. It said something like, "Thank the Lord Jesus Christ for He told me to give you the rollerblades."

I took my guitar out of the trunk and climbed the tower overlooking the beach to praise the Lord which was my custom. When I came down from the tower, I saw the college student from Arizona State. He skated over to me and he said, "I have to tell you something". I nodded my head as to say go ahead. He said, "Do you know that today is my birthday? My mom brought me here for my birthday, but what I really wanted for my birthday was a set of rollerblades." Then he paused while looking at me and said, "I never met a Christian man like you."

Chapter 3

2 Timothy 1:6-10
6 Wherefore I put thee in remembrance that thou stir up the gift of God, which is in thee by the putting on of my hands. 7 For God hath not given us the spirit of fear; but of power, and of love, and of a sound mind. 8 Be not thou therefore ashamed of the testimony of our Lord, nor of me his prisoner: but be thou partaker of the afflictions of the gospel according to the power of God; 9 Who hath saved us, and called[us] with an holy calling, not according to our works, but according to his own purpose and grace, which was given us in Christ Jesus before the world began, 10 But is now made manifest by the appearing of our Saviour Jesus Christ, who hath abolished death, and hath brought life and immortality to light through the gospel:

God has called us with a holy calling, not according to our works, but according to his own purpose and grace.

I gave up everything I had through the process of going to Bible College and into the mission field. It was nothing compared to the hope that God had placed in my heart in Christ Jesus.

People like stuff and stuff can get in the way of God's purpose, and I'm no different than the next guy. I like my stuff, but it wasn't as important as the calling God had placed upon my life. There is nothing wrong in possessing things, but sometimes our stuff can get in the way of God's plan for our life. So, I had to give up all I had to pursue the calling that God had placed on my life.

I moved to Denver, Colorado. I secured a room at the Bible College, and I was surprised to find out that it was in a shopping mall along with the church.

There are three things that I remember most about Bible College. The first was a hermeneutics exam, the second was witnessing, and the third was receiving my first passport.

First, I remember that hermeneutics was a very hard course for everyone at the Bible college. Just before the exam everyone was studying very hard. The students were uncertain about how well they would do on the exam.

At some point, I decided I wasn't going to worry anymore. It is written:

1 Peter 5:7
Casting all your care upon him; for he careth for you.

I casted all my cares on the Lord!

So, I started to pray and ask God for His help on the exam. I prayed until I received a word that I would get a good grade on the exam. This word was followed by a peace. This peace would manifest itself during and after the exam.

The day of the exam came; everybody still had their faces in their books while they were waiting for the exam to start. I just sat quietly looking around the room with a smile on my face. I noticed that the professor was looking at me. Probably because I was the only one who seemed relaxed about the exam.

We took the exam, and after we finished, we met outside the classroom. Everyone seemed sad. However, I was laughing and dancing with joy in the hallway. The professor came out and saw me dancing. Again, he noticed that I had a different attitude toward the exam than other students.

A few days later, we received our exam grades. The whole class did poorly. My grade was a D+, but I didn't believe it would be my final grade. I was very happy because I had a word from God. His word on the situation was more real than anything I was facing.

The professor wanted to know why I was filled with joy during the exam process. I told him something like, "God is bigger than this exam".

The next time we came to class the professor announced that he had adjusted the grades according to some type of curve. My grade became a B. God delivered on His word, and I received a good grade on my hermeneutics exam.

Whenever I look back on this testimony, I'm reminded how important it is to look at Jesus, the author and finisher of my faith, while I'm standing. In addition, it reminds me of how to act even when the circumstances are contrary to what I've prayed, and to stand in God's strength which is an important element of the standing process.

Second, witnessing with fellow Bible College students was not exactly what I thought it would be. It was very hard to get anyone to go out witnessing. The main reason is obvious. Students attend classes and must study, in addition to working part-time and full-time jobs. Therefore, many students lack the ambition to do anything extra.

However, I found a good witnessing partner in Joe Cima. Also, there was a student from India named Abraham who would go witnessing with me occasionally. Our favorite witnessing spots were supermarkets and malls.

There were two events that I remember the most concerning my witnessing during my time at Bible College. The first was when Joe and I went to the local supermarket to witness.

Joe was one of the best I've ever seen at street witnessing. He was very confident and he new how to talk with people and deal with whatever their objections were. He helped many people to receive Jesus as their savior.

However, this one time, Joe and I were witnessing at the supermarket when he had a disagreement with this women over her groceries. It all began with the friendly act of Joe wanting to help the women, but she didn't want to be helped.

What happened next, I can only describe as a tug of war. Now! There is Joe determined to help this women, and this women that was determined not to be helped. I looked at this whole incident in unbelief for a few seconds before I decided to help the women get her groceries back from Joe.

Joe looked at me with that infectious smile he was always wearing and we both started to laugh. We laughed and laughed knowing that God was greater than our mistakes. After that, we went back to telling everyone we met about Jesus knowing that He gave the increase.

The second witnessing event, that I recall, happened when I was with Abraham and Joe. We went to the shopping mall to witness when we saw an ambulance and police cars at the mall.

I started to talk to some teenagers and young adults nearby, and I asked them what happened. They stated there was a fight and their friend was hurt, and he was in the ambulance.

I told them, "I know what to do". I asked them to gather around me, and I had them pray for their friend. Next, I ask them, "Who needs to receive Jesus as their savior"? Most of them responded favorably, and I led them in prayer to receive Jesus as their personal savior.

I believed this was a Divine appointment. We were in the right place, at the right time, with the right people.

As far as witnessing, there were certain things I learned through the process of following the Holy Spirit (the true Witness). There are keys in every culture and in every group of society that open the doors to evangelism.

There is a good example of this in the book of acts (17:23-34) Paul was able to use an alter dedicated to an unknown God to preach the Gospel.

Acts 17:23-34
23 For as I passed by, and beheld your devotions, I found an altar with this inscription, TO THE UNKNOWN God. Whom therefore ye ignorantly worship, him declare I unto you. 24 God that made the world and all things therein, seeing that he is Lord of heaven and earth, dwelleth not in temples made with hands; 25 Neither is worshipped with men's hands, as though he needed any thing, seeing he giveth to all life, and breath, and all things; 26 And hath made of one blood all nations of men for to dwell on all the face of the earth, and hath determined the times before appointed, and the bounds of their habitation; 27 That they should seek the Lord, if

haply they might feel after him, and find him, though he be not far from every one of us: 28 For in him we live, and move, and have our being; as certain also of your own poets have said, For we are also his offspring. 29 Forasmuch then as we are the offspring of God, we ought not to think that the Godhead is like unto gold, or silver, or stone, graven by art and man's device. 30 And the times of this ignorance God winked at; but now commandeth all men every where to repent: 31 Because he hath appointed a day, in the which he will judge the world in righteousness by[that] man whom he hath ordained;[whereof] he hath given assurance unto all[men], in that he hath raised him from the dead. 32 And when they heard of the resurrection of the dead, some mocked: and others said, We will hear thee again of this[matter]. 33 So Paul departed from among them. 34 Howbeit certain men clave unto him, and believed: among the which[was] Dionysius the Areopagite, and a woman named Damaris, and others with them.

One of the keys that I found to be successful in today's cultures is to use TV shows and movies that are popular as a means of connecting with the listener. People who would not listen to you preach the gospel strait out may talk to you about a movie or TV show.

One of the movies I liked to use for witnessing was the motion picture *Contact*.

Here are the last few lines of this movie (*Contact*, 1997).

"Do you know about the scientific concept known as Occam's razor?
Yes! It means all things being equal the simplest explanation tends to be the right one.

You come to us with no evidence no record, no artifacts, only a story to put it mildly strains credibility. Why don't you withdraw your testimony and concede the fact that this testimony never took place?

Because I can't!
I had an experience.
I can't prove it.
I can't explain it.
Everything I know as a human being.
Everything that I am tells me it was real.
I was given something wonderful.
Something that changed me forever.
A vision of the universe that tells us how tiny and significant and how rare and precious we are..

A vision that tells us we belong to something greater than ourselves

That none of us are alone.

I wish I could share that.

I wish.

I wish that everyone for one moment could feel that awe and humility and hope.

That continues to be my wish."

P. Gruber & L. Obst (Producers) & R. Zemeckis (Director). 1997. *Contact* [Motion Picture]. United States: Warner Brothers.

What ideas came to your mind when you read these words? I used it as an open door to talk about my experience with Christ. I never had a problem with people not wanting to hear about it, and I usually finished with praying in agreement with them that they would receive an experience from God.

Another key that opens people to the gospel of Jesus Christ is music. I was riding on a Grey Hound bus when a man in his 20's started rapping. After he had finished, I said, "I can rap better than that." He said, "Let's hear it!" I rapped the song "Jesus Loves Me".

JaJa Jesus loves me this I know
For the Bible tells me so
Little ones to him belong
They are weak
But he is strong
Yes! Jesus loves me
Yes! Jesus loves me
Yes! Jesus loves me
the Bible tells me so

When I finished, there were a lot of cheers. Many people told me that I did the best. However, what was important was people heard about the love of Jesus and enjoyed it. They weren't inconvenienced or dragged into a conversation they didn't what to be involved in.

Again, the Holy Spirit is the true witness who can show you the best way to witness in the situation you're facing. Remember, Jesus did what he saw the Father do (John 5:19).

Third, I had put in an application for my passport during the time I was at Bible College. Whether I did it just before I entered Bible College, or just after I entered

Bible College, I don't remember. What I do remember is receiving my passport.

I check my mailbox everyday in anticipation of receiving my passport. It was something I looked forward to have in my possession. I don't even remember why it was so important for me to have it, but I knew it was something I needed. Let's say God put it on my heart to get one.

Then that wonderful day came. I received my passport. I was filled with unspeakable joy. I started running around the Bible College like a little kid telling everyone I just received my passport. I'm sure I look like a child that had received the Christmas present that he had longed for so much. I was filled with an illuminating happiness from above, and it showed as I told everyone about my new passport.

This went on for several minutes. Many believers responded with congratulations, and I'm happy for you. However, someone asked me, "Where are you going?" That's when the wind went out of my sails. Until someone asked that question, there were a plethora of possibilities running through my mind. But, now! I had to face this question. So, I answered, "I don't know".

Then I had to ask myself, "Why am I so excited and what happened to my excitement?" The answer lies in the seen and unseen. I was seeing the invisible until someone introduced the visible. When I started to look at the visible, the invisible faded away until it disappeared.

2 Corinthians 4:18
So we fix our eyes not on what is seen, but what is unseen. For what is seen is temporary, but what is unseen is eternal.

Chapter 4

Somewhere in the middle of the first semester of Bible College I started to go to a church in Aurora, Colorado. The Pastor was a Korean woman. The church was also a mission that helped the homeless. I was interested in the mission work done in the church because I had seen how bad the homeless situation was in Denver when I was witnessing, and I wanted to do something about it. Therefore, I took noticed that here was a church doing something about the situation.

I went to college with the Pastor's daughter, and she invited me to this church. After seeing the church, I started to pray that Jesus would help them, and He placed it upon my heart to return.

The following week, Mary K. Baxter (The author of "Devine Revelation of Hell") was speaking at the church. I attended the service, and Mary K. Baxter called me to the front of the church. She laid hands on me and prophesied that I had a great calling on my life.

Two weeks later, I was asked to come to the church in a leadership position. I was given the title of mission director, and placed in charge of the homeless ministry.

Note:
Just before this period of time, I was down to $26.00, and I placed the money in the collection plate. The next night I wrote an I.O.U. For thirty dollars; I placed it in the bucket. Two days later I went through my car and found enough change to do my laundry. I was broke, but then something wonderful happened. Later in the afternoon, I received a check for approximately $2,500.00; I received another check for approximately $1000.00 two days later. I paid the thirty dollar I.O.U.

Homeless ministry
For almost six months, I lived with the homeless. I ate with them. I slept where they slept, I laughed with them, and I cried with them.

I taught recovery class on Tuesday night. The class never had more than 7 people, but they were seven of the most interesting people I've met. They were dealing with alcohol, drug, homosexuality, physical abuse, rape, and demonization.

Almost every service there was something going on. The church was in an area infested by drug addicts. Prostitutes were on almost every street and so was crime. The area was a war zone, and we were "Fort Church". I was threatened with harm several times by the inhabitants of that area.

One service, a man yelled at the Pastor, and he became very violent. We subdued him and dragged him out of the church. This man tried to come back into the church and struck one of the ushers in the face in the process. The usher fought with the man until we subdued both of them.

Then the pastor's husband tried to cast the devil out of the belligerent man while the man was spitting on him. The result was the man eventually calmed down.

After that, we escorted him outside again, and this time he didn't try to come back into the church.

This type of incident would repeat itself in difference ways. Once we were witnessing and had brought a group of armed Satanist to the church. We never feared them even when threats were made. We were kind to them, told them about Jesus, and fed them. They left without hurting anyone. Also, we had members of the church who were threaten or assaulted by those they were helping. There were no major injuries, and everyone operated in God's love and forgiveness no matter what situation they were facing.

One night during a prayer meeting, the Pastor noticed a man wasn't acting right. She asked me to escort him out of the meeting. I approached the man and notice I could only see the whites of his eyes. I could not see any pupils or retinas, only white. Also, he was walking back and forth in some kind of response to the prayer.

I looked up and said, "Jesus! This one is yours". I placed myself between the man and others. He tried to spit on me but nothing would come out of his mouth but air.

After a couple of minutes, the man turned and walked toward the door, but he stopped before going out the door. I looked up and said, "Jesus you always finish what you start. Jesus, thank you for finishing the job". Then the man stepped through the door; his eyes began to flutter, his pupils returned, and he walked away. "Praise the Lord!" I said as I went back into the meeting.

Witnessing

I would go witnessing with Joe (chapter 3) and believers from different area churches, as well as believers from the church that I attended. We would normally go to the sixteenth street mall area in downtown Denver, Colorado. We would witness to gang members, Satanist, witches, street people, and everyone else who would listen to what we had to say about the kingdom of God.

One day we were witnessing when the rear guard of a satanic cult took my picture. I ran up to the man and gave him my business card. The man didn't want to be touched by the card. He started to run from me yelling for the police. The police were right there, but they didn't respond to the man's call for help.

I walked away wondering why this man was so afraid of my business card. That's when the Lord whispered to me, "They are covered in the blood of Jesus." The Holy Spirit revealed to me the mighty power of the blood of Jesus. Demonic spirits fear the blood, and it was brought to my remembrance that I had prayed the blood of Jesus over the cards. Praise the Lord for His precious blood. Amen!

Joe and I were witnessing another time at the sixteenth street mall when we saw a teenage boy standing by himself at a bus stop. Joe approached him and started to talk to him as I began to pray. The teenager received Jesus as his savior.

After rejoicing with our new brother, we went searching for the other team we were working with at the mall. We were searching for them for approximately half an hour when we saw the teen age boy again. This time he was with a group of his friends. We walked closer and realized that they were a gang. It didn't stop us from talking to them about Jesus. The whole gang received Jesus as their savior, and we prayed with them. "What a night!" I thought.

Michael and Michael

I first met Michael#1 witnessing. He was standing in front of a liquor store bumming money for a drink. I prayed with Michael and another man. I took them to a store that had food, and I bought them something to eat.

I saw Michael a few weeks later in our soup line. I talked with him about Jesus. He would disappear from our soup line and come back from time to time. The pull of the street kept him out of reach for awhile.

One Sunday, during church service, the Lord spoke to my heart, "Go outside!" I walked outside; I saw Michael sitting on the sidewalk crying. I said, "Where do you think you can hide from God". He replied, "I don't know!"

Michael wanted to stop drinking, and he asked me to help him. Michael became my companion around the church. The Lord touched Michael, and he was good at fixing things that needed mending around the church.

Michael#2 came to the church on Christmas day. He was crying and he needed someone to talk to him. The church staff was having a Christmas party and we were instructed to let no one in, but somewhere inside me I heard, "Help him!" I could not turn him away.

I did not see Michael#2 for a couple of days. He came to Sunday service and the Pastor laid hands on him during prayer. Immediately, there was a strange smell that departed from Michael#2. The smell started to move around the room, and you could see its movement by the looks on peoples' faces. Whatever it was, it was moving around the room as though it was searching for something or someone before it appeared to leave the building.

Both Michaels were doing well on their sobriety. So, I took them out to eat and celebrated their victory in

Christ. They experienced a few weeks of peace and growth in the Lord. They became good friends and encouraged one another in Christ.

However, the enemy was not ready to quit. Michael#2 had an ex-wife who wanted him to come back to her and their daughter. Unfortunately, she had a drinking problem and coming back to her would interfere with his recovery. Michael knew he had to get his life in order before he could deal with the problems in his family.

His ex-wife and brother came into the church highly intoxicated and tried to get Michael to leave. We formed a protective barrier around Michael because they started to get violent and tried to physically drag him out of the church. They wanted him to go drinking with them and to forget the church nonsense.

His family left the church and started to vandalize vehicles in the parking lot. They continued to beat on the door and harassed people who were entering and exiting the church. They would not go away.

Inside the church we were praying for them. Meanwhile, Michael#2's brother called the police, and the police came and took him and Michael's ex-wife away. That wasn't the result they were looking for, but it was an answer to our prayers.

Unfortunately, Michael caved in to the constant pressure that his family put on him to leave the church. After almost two months of being sober, Michael started drinking again.

The Book of Nehemiah (Nehemiah 6:17-19) gives us an example of how Satan will use your family against you. Michael was learning this lesson the hard way. I prayed that the light of Jesus Christ would bring him back out of the blackness. Amen!

Michael and Michael became good friends, so shortly after Michael#2 fell so did Michael#1. They both went back to the streets. It's my hope to see them out of that hell in this life or the next. If you are reading this book Michael and Michael, God loves you and so do I.

The enemy within (self)
the pastor was very demanding at times, but I enjoyed doing the work I was assigned. One of my assignments was to talk with those who were leaving the church and convince them to stay if at all possible. I was able to convince someone to stay on one occasion, but other than that, everyone wanted to go because they thought the pastor was too controlling.

People would leave and the control issue came up again and again. I talked to another believer about it and he loaned me his book that was written by Roberts Liardon. I don't remember the title of the book, but it was about controlling spirits in the church. There were questions in the book that could help you determine if controlling spirits were present in the church.

The book gave me an understanding that there was a problem with a spirit of control in the church, but I didn't know what to do about it right away.

I knew as a leader in the church that I had to confront this issue. So, I talk to the pastor about what I had learned from Roberts Liardon's book on controlling spirits. The pastor made it clear that there would be no more discussions on this issue, and I was stripped of my position right on the spot.

I prayed for weeks on what to do. During this period, I saw a vision. I saw an upside down pentagram on the church altar. I knew that if I would stay there - there would be strife. So, I understood in my heart it was time to go.

Matthew 5:25-26
25 Agree with thine adversary quickly, whiles thou art in the way with him; lest at any time the adversary deliver thee to the judge, and the judge deliver thee to the officer, and thou be cast into prison. 26 Verily I say unto thee, Thou shalt by no means come out thence, till thou hast paid the uttermost farthing.

    When my decision to leave was final, I went to the pastor and asked for her forgiveness and apologized. She wanted me to stay, but I believed God was leading me down a different road.
    I spent the next three months pressing in to God's presence. I spent hours in fellowship every day. I would pray in the mornings, and I would ride my bike to a nearby lake after prayer. I would reflect on my prayers and meditate on scripture.
    At the beginning of this period I tried to promote my friend Abraham's plans for a mission trip, but I could not raise a penny for him. Also, I made other mistakes while I was trying to dot every "i" and cross every "t" of my faith at the time.
    I heard a man say, "When a man works, a man works, but when a man prays, God works". So, I got busy praying. However, the answer wasn't what I expected. God put it on my heart to ask Abraham for his forgiveness and to be released from my promise. Abraham released me from my promise, and I went back to praying.

Chapter 5

—◊—

Matthew 18:2-6
2 And Jesus called a little child unto him, and set him in the midst of them, 3 And said, Verily I say unto you, Except ye be converted, and become as little children, ye shall not enter into the kingdom of heaven. 4 Whosoever therefore shall humble himself as this little child, the same is greatest in the kingdom of heaven. 5 And whoso shall receive one such little child in my name receiveth me. 6 But whoso shall offend one of these little ones which believe in me, it were better for him that a millstone were hanged about his neck, and[that] he were drowned in the depth of the sea.

Jesus called a little child unto him, and set him in the mist of them. I felt like a little child at Christmas time when I received my passport. I didn't know where I was going, but I knew I was going, and I was full of joy thinking about it. Within a few weeks, I was introduced to David Clifton (president and founder of David Clifton Ministries). He heard about my music writing abilities, and he came to interview me for his radio show.

The day of the interview David had to go to a funeral in Colorado Springs. So, since it looked like he was not coming, I invited my friend Bill over. My roommate Joe

Cima was there too when David knocked surprisingly on the door.

David didn't come for the reason I thought. He was looking for people to go on the mission trip to China with him. I told him that I had two thousand dollars set aside for a mission trip. David said, "You will have to raise $2,700.00 to be able to go on the mission trip. Bill and Joe both spoke up. Each one stated that they would pay half of the $700.00 that I needed for the trip. This was a lot of money for both of these men at that time.

My prayers were answered. God brought everything I needed to go on a mission trip to my home that day. "When man works, man works, but when man prays, God works."

At this time, I want to impart the wisdom that God showed me through His scripture and through others who were there for me. I was in the midst of believers who were raising the child named "Robert". When I (the child named Robert) grew up in Christ I taught these basic beliefs that I learned from others.

Discipleship.

Discipline.
Individual
Seeking
Christ
In
Power
Loving
Everyone
Showing.
Holiness
In.
presence

Disciplined

God has a way of working the bugs out of our lives. We submit to him and move toward His rest. Each situation we face and every decision we make is a test either moving us closer or further away from Christ.

We suffer as He suffered and we grow closer in relationship. Suffering has a way of helping us to press in. We learn to seek Him instead of ourselves. We learn to lean on the source of all things. Discipleship works the enemy out of the equation.

The student is the disciple. The disciple is seeking to become one with God almighty. A student or disciple can only become as great as his mentor. If our mentor is man, we are limited. If our mentor is God, we have infinite possibilities for nothing is impossible with God. The mentor is God's Holy Spirit.

Hebrews 8:10-11
10 For this[is] the covenant that I will make with the house of Israel after those days, saith the Lord; I will put my laws into their mind, and write them in their hearts: and I will be to them a God, and they shall be to me a people: 11 And they shall not teach every man his neighbour, and every man his brother, saying, Know the Lord: for all shall know me, from the least to the greatest.

1 John 2:20
20 But ye have an unction from the Holy One, and ye know all things.

1 John 2:27-29
27 But the anointing which ye have received of him abideth in you, and ye need not that any man teach you: but as the same anointing teacheth you of all

things, and is truth, and is no lie, and even as it hath taught you, ye shall abide in him. 28 And now, little children, abide in him; that, when he shall appear, we may have confidence, and not be ashamed before him at his coming. 29 If ye know that he is righteous, ye know that every one that doeth righteousness is born of him.

The Lord develops us and matures us in Christ so we can become physical examples of His love. These physical examples or mentors point us into relationship with Christ, and help equip us for ministry.

1 Corinthians 4:13-21
13 Being defamed, we intreat: we are made as the filth of the world,[and are] the offscouring of all things unto this day. 14 I write not these things to shame you, but as my beloved sons I warn[you]. 15 For though ye have ten thousand instructors in Christ, yet[have ye] not many fathers: for in Christ Jesus I have begotten you through the gospel. 16 Wherefore I beseech you, be ye followers of me. 17 For this cause have I sent unto you Timotheus, who is my beloved son, and faithful in the Lord, who shall bring you into remembrance of my ways which be in Christ, as I teach every where in every church. 18 Now some are puffed up, as though I would not come to you. 19 But I will come to you shortly, if the Lord will, and will know, not the speech of them which are puffed up, but the power. 20 For the kingdom of God[is] not in word, but in power. 21 What will ye? shall I come unto you with a rod, or in love, and[in] the spirit of meekness?

The Lord's power is His precious Holy Spirit. God's Holy Spirit trains us from within and he places believers filled with His Holy Spirit to fellowship with us and encourage us to do what we are called to do.

We learn discipleship through fellowship and we are tested in what we have learned by the situations that are placed in our lives. These situations cause us to move closer to God and His peace and rest, or move away from God. However, the internal and external mentor works to encourage us to continue in the process.

Titus 2:11-12
11 For the grace of God that bringeth salvation hath appeared to all men, 12 Teaching us that, denying ungodliness and worldly lusts, we should live soberly, righteously, and godly, in this present world;

We are disciplined through His grace. God is in every part of this process. Everyone is a student and a mentor in Christ.

Student
Luke 6:40

Mentor
1 Corinthians 4:13-21
Luke 10:27

Individual
1 Corinthians 12:12-26
12 For as the body is one, and hath many members, and all the members of that one body, being many, are one body: so also[is] Christ. 13 For by one Spirit are we all baptized into one body, whether[we be] Jews or Gentiles, whether[we be] bond or free; and have been all made to drink into one Spirit. 14 For the body

is not one member, but many. 15 If the foot shall say, Because I am not the hand, I am not of the body; is it therefore not of the body? 16 And if the ear shall say, Because I am not the eye, I am not of the body; is it therefore not of the body? 17 If the whole body[were] an eye, where[were] the hearing? If the whole[were] hearing, where[were] the smelling? 18 But now hath God set the members every one of them in the body, as it hath pleased him. 19 And if they were all one member, where[were] the body? 20 But now[are they] many members, yet but one body. 21 And the eye cannot say unto the hand, I have no need of thee: nor again the head to the feet, I have no need of you. 22 Nay, much more those members of the body, which seem to be more feeble, are necessary: 23 And those[members] of the body, which we think to be less honourable, upon these we bestow more abundant honour; and our uncomely[parts] have more abundant comeliness. 24 For our comely[parts] have no need: but God hath tempered the body together, having given more abundant honour to that[part] which lacked: 25 That there should be no schism in the body; but[that] the members should have the same care one for another. 26 And whether one member suffer, all the members suffer with it; or one member be honoured, all the members rejoice with it.

    We are individuals who are in relationship with our heavenly father. We seek Him with all our heart, soul, strength, and mind.

    He feeds us our daily bread. God directs us toward His will and purpose for our lives. We find out our position in the body of Christ through Him, and we work with others who the Holy Spirit has placed in our path to fulfill our individual purposes and callings. In other words, we work together as one, but we are also individuals with specific instructions and duties from God.

Seeking
Matthew 7:7-8
7 Ask, and it shall be given you; seek, and ye shall find; knock, and it shall be opened unto you: 8 For every one that asketh receiveth; and he that seeketh findeth; and to him that knocketh it shall be opened.

He who seeks finds. It's the seeker who finds what he or she is looking for. It's guaranteed in God's word. We are to be seeking God who is truth. Jesus said, "I'm the way, the truth and the life".
Knowledge, wisdom and understanding are revealed to us by this seeking process. Prayer, praise, reading and meditating on God's word, as well as fellowship and learning from the experience of other believers are all part of this seeking process.

Christ
I learned in church,
"The Son of God became the son of man so the sons of men could become the sons of God".
Christ means "anointed one". Jesus was anointed of God going about healing and freeing those who were oppressed by the devil. His mission was to do the will of God. Jesus did what he was told unto the death of the cross. Jesus said only what the father said.

Attributes of Christ
    Belief toward God.   Heb. 11:6
    Holiness toward God.   Heb 12:10,14
    Godliness.   Titus 2:12

Called

Love.	Matt 22:36,37
	1 Cor 13:1-13
Faith.	Mark 11:22
	2 Tim 1:12
Joy.	Phil 4:4
Worship.	Phil 2:4-11
Obedience.	2 thess 1:8
Imitation.	1 Cor 11:1
Fellowship.	1 John 1:3
Walk.	Gal 5:16
Infilling	Eph 5:18
Guided.	John 16:13
Praying.	Jude 1:20
Don't quench.	1 Thess 5:19
Taught.	John 14:26
Living.	Gal 5:25
Don't grieve.	Eph 4:30
Chastity.	1 Tim 5:22
Contentment.	Heb 13:5
Diligence	1 Thess 3:7,8
Forbearance	Eph 4:2
Honesty.	Eph 4:25
Industry.	1 Thess 4:11,12
Enemies.	Matt 5:44
Peacefulness	Rom 14:17-19
Temperance.	1 cor 9:25
Tolerance.	Rom 14:1-23
Good deeds.	Titus 2:14
Bearing burdens.	Gal 6:2
Helping others.	Acts 11:29,30
Fellowship.	Acts 2:42
Kindness.	1 Pet 4:7-11
	Col 3:12,13
Humility.	1 Pet 5:5,6
Edification.	1 Thess 5:11

Spiritual growth.	2 Pet 3:18
Fruitfulness.	Jn 15:1-6
Perseverance.	1 Cor 15:58
Persecution.	2 Tim 3:9-12
Obedience.	Phil 2:12
Good works.	James 2:14-26
Gentleness	James 3:17,18
Self control.	Gal 5:23
Peace.	Phil. 4:27

Christ like character is more than knowing who you are in Christ. True character is revealing the love of Christ even when you are persecuted by others.

In
In Christ is relationship. First you are in relationship with God. You love him with all your heart, soul, strength, and mind. His love flows through your relationship with Him. You share your relationship with God with your brothers and sisters in Christ. They share their relationship with God with you. You go forth in ministry and share God's love with the world.

In Christ His attributes are imparted.
In relationship his character is seen.
In fellowship He is revealed to others.
In ministry He is known by the world.

Power
God's Holy Spirit gives us power.

Acts 1:8
But ye shall receive power, after that the Holy Ghost is come upon you: and ye shall be witnesses unto me both in Jerusalem, and in all Judaea, and in Samaria, and unto the uttermost part of the earth.

The Gospel of Jesus Christ is to be presented in power. The power of Christ flows through our lives making an impact on others we meet.

Loving everyone
Matthew 5:43-48
43 Ye have heard that it hath been said, Thou shalt love thy neighbour, and hate thine enemy. 44 But I say unto you, Love your enemies, bless them that curse you, do good to them that hate you, and pray for them which despitefully use you, and persecute you; 45 That ye may be the children of your Father which is in heaven: for he maketh his sun to rise on the evil and on the good, and sendeth rain on the just and on the unjust. 46 For if ye love them which love you, what reward have ye? do not even the publicans the same? 47 And if ye salute your brethren only, what do ye more[than others]? do not even the publicans so? 48 Be ye therefore perfect, even as your Father which is in heaven is perfect.

A disciple is a discipline individual seeking Christ in power loving everyone. A disciple is also part of the body of Christ and a follower of the Holy Spirit and the Word of God. Once you are filled with His knowledge and love you start showing others that His holiness is present in your life.

Showing
Paul said, "For though ye have ten thousand instructors in Christ, yet [have ye] not many fathers: for in Christ Jesus I have begotten you through the gospel. Wherefore I beseech you, be ye followers of me (1 Corinthians 4:15, 16)."

Holiness
Hebrews 12:24
Follow peace with all [men], and holiness, without which no man shall see the Lord.

We are to put on the new man, which after God is created in righteousness and true holiness (Ephesians 4:24).

In presence
1 Corinthians 1:29-31
That no flesh should glory in his presence. But of him are ye in Christ Jesus, who of God is made unto us wisdom, and righteousness, and sanctification, and redemption: That, according as it is written, He that glorieth, let him glory in the Lord.

Jesus did many great things in the presence of his disciples (John 20:30).

SHIP
(Discipleship, Mentorship, and Leadership)
Psalms 127:
1 Except the Lord build the house, they labour in vain that build it: except the LORD keep the city, the watchman waketh[but] in vain.

    We as leaders are called to show God's holiness in presence. When you are in relationship with God, His attributes show up in your live in increasing measure.
    A mentor is someone who knows his Father, and his Father is known by those who know him. He walks in love.

Acts 2:17-21
17 And it shall come to pass in the last days, saith God, I will pour out of my Spirit upon all flesh: and your sons and your daughters shall prophesy, and your young men shall see visions, and your old men shall dream dreams: 18 And on my servants and on my handmaidens I will pour out in those days of my Spirit; and they shall prophesy: 19 And I will shew wonders in heaven above, and signs in the earth beneath; blood, and fire, and vapour of smoke: 20 The sun shall be turned into darkness, and the moon into blood, before that great and notable day of the Lord come: 21 And it shall come to pass,[that] whosoever shall call on the name of the Lord shall be saved.

A leader prophecies the word of God into believers' lives, Edifies and exhorts believers, as well as helps them to connect with God's will and purpose for their lives. Discipleship is cooperation between God and His people. Discipleship is cooperation between mentors and students. Discipleship is a family raising one another in love.

Back to the China mission trip:
The china team prayed together and witnessed together on the streets of Denver before we went to China. We already had a good idea of our strengths and weaknesses, and where we fit into the team.

In China, we passed out all the tracks and delivered all the Bibles. I do not want to go into detail because there are many brothers and sisters in Christ that maybe put in harm's way.

The team was on a Christian TV show after we all came back from the mission trip. We talked about the many things that God was doing in China.

In addition, two team members and I went to Vietnam and delivered Christian bibles and other materials to the church in Hanoi. We also went to Hong Kong and witnessed to people during the British/ Chinese ceremony which transferred the rule of Hong Kong back to the Chinese.

Chapter 6

1 Corinthians 1:26
For ye see your calling, brethren, how that not many wise men after the flesh, not many mighty, not many noble,[are called]:

While I was on the China mission trip, a word came to me that I was going to Khayalitcha. I had the same enthusiasm that I had when I received my passport. I told everyone on the mission trip that I was going to Khayalitcha. Most people seemed less enthused than I did. However, I remained happy knowing that I was going on another mission trip soon.

Within two weeks after my return from China, I was on the plane for Johannesburg, South Africa. After landing, I went to retrieve my luggage only to find that my suit case was damaged beyond all repair. The South African Airline representative gave me a certificate for a new one.

I walked through customs, and I proceeded out of customs into the other side of the airport before I realized that I had passed through customs without being checked. I walked back into customs, and I had to search for someone. I finally found a male custom official that said," you're ok. Go!" I was happy because if they would have search me, they would have found that I didn't have no where near the money I needed to stay in South Africa for three months. I was depending on God to supply my every need.

I waited in the airport for hours for someone to walk up to me and say the Lord sent me, but no such person came. There was a taxi-driver that kept asking me if he could take me somewhere. Finally, after a long period of time, maybe 2-3 hours, I went with the taxi-driver.

I had $140.00 on me for the trip. The cab driver charged me R120 and the hotel he took me to charged R250 for one night. This was approximately $90.00. I was still hoping that provision from the Lord would manifest soon.

I went straight to my room and immediately got into bed. I slept until midnight. When I woke up, I started praying and praising the Lord. I didn't want to be defeated by doubt or unbelief at this stage. I was at the point of no return. I was committed to the call I heard. After putting my face to the floor and crying out to the Lord for help, I kept hearing to look in the free tourist magazine that I picked up at the airport. So, I looked through the magazine and an advertisement for a backpacker place called something like "The Castle" caught my eye. However, I was not sure why it caught my eye, because I thought the Lord was going to deliver me from this situation by using other believers.

The next morning I checked out of the hotel; I took a taxi to the luggage store to replace my broken suitcase. For some reason, it took several hours for them to replace the suit case. Meanwhile, I started to think maybe the owner of the luggage store was going to help me. I started dropping hints, and so did they. They put their phone in front of me suggesting that I should make a phone call.

I knew my back was against the wall. It was time for God to come through because I didn't have a place to go. That's when I started thinking about the backpacker place again. I opened the magazine and found the phone number. I called them, and they said that they would pick me up. After an hour of them not being able to locate me, I decided to take a taxi.

No sooner than when I got into a taxi, a knife fight broke out in the street.

Two men ran in front of the taxi. One man passed a long knife to another man standing next to him. Then I heard a war scream rise up from a man that was standing on the opposite side of the street. The screaming man had a similar knife in his hand, and he was waving it in the air as he ran at the man that just received the long knife in front of the taxi. The taxi-driver sped away before it got too ugly.

I worked as a military police officer, deputy sheriff and a correction officer for a total of thirteen years. During all that time, I never saw a knife fight in progress. I witnessed the results of such things, but I never saw it actually happen. Wow! I was in South Africa less than one day, and I had already seen violence.

When I got to "The Castle"(hostel), I took the rest of my money and paid for as many nights as I could. I had enough money to stay 10 nights. This would keep me off the streets for a week and a half, and give me time to fast and pray for God's direction.

There were two men in the room when I entered. One man was lying down and the other man identified himself as Dave.

There were three sets of bunks that were stacked three beds high. While taking off my shoes, I placed my hands on the third bunk, and felt money on the bunk. I asked everyone in the room if they had lost any money, and they all said, "no"! They both left the room a few minutes later, and I scooped the money off the bed. It was more than enough to feed me for the next few days. I didn't have to fast if I didn't want to.

Later in the evening, Dave came back and told me that he was robbed while he was site-seeing. He needed to stay at the hostel two more nights before going to Cape Town. I had enough money from the "bed of money" to pay for his two nights and still have several meals.

Dave went to church with me, and he renewed his commitment to God. I told him that I was going to Khayalitcha; Dave told me that he was going to Cape Town which is close to Khayalitcha. So, he volunteered to prepare the way for me to go to Khayalitcha when he got to Cape Town.

During my stay at the castle I told many people about Jesus. The Lord put the manager, Irwin, on my heart, and I prayed for him and witnessed to him constantly. Irwin came from Austria, and his philosophy was smoke dope, drink beer, make money, and smoke more dope.

The breakthrough came when the Lord told me to give Irwin my belt buckle. I gave Irwin the belt buckle and he went into another room. He came back with a belt that had a broken buckle. Irwin's heart started to melt. He asked me some questions. I sat in the bar, which was located inside the hostel, witnessing to him. He would hear what I'm saying, but he didn't really listen. He acknowledged that what I was doing was important but not for him.

I kept after Irwin. Sometimes he would retaliate by blowing pot smoke in my face, but I wouldn't let it discourage me. I knew that God had a plan for Irwin and whether he received it or not, while I was with him, wasn't important. The important thing was planting seeds and turning the other cheek.

While I was witnessing to Irwin, he started to allow things that he would not allow at first. He let me play praise songs on my guitar in the hostel's bar and bring in Christian CDs which he played. Later, I was allowed to preach in the bar. That's right! Church was happening in the bar, and there were some that listened and there were some who did not. It didn't matter to me, as long as I was talking about Jesus seeds were being planted.

It's important to understand the we are part of a team, and all we have to do is our part. Someone else will come along and do their part until God's will is accomplished. I believed for everyone's salvation that heard my preaching. Whether they received it then or later in their lives, I had already released the belief when I spoke. It doesn't matter who plants and who waters as long as someone is planting and someone is watering. It's God who gives the increase.

After Dave went to Cape Town, Gary came to The Castle. Gary believed in Jesus, but he wasn't attending church. We became quick friends.

God gave me a word for Gary. Gary would come with me to Cape Town. However, Gary showed no desire to go to Cape Town.

A couple of days before my 10 nights lodging at The Castle were complete, I received funds from America. I went to the train station and bought two 2nd class tickets for Cape Town.

I told Gary the second ticket was for him, but he told me that he didn't want to go. I let him know the word I received from God and that I bought the ticket in faith. Gary thought it was funny because he didn't want to go to Cape Town.

The day came for me to leave for Cape Town. Gary was packed and ready to go. He still wasn't sure if he was going, but the idea was starting to appeal to him. Gary changed his mind several times. He even remarked a few times on the way to the train that he was not going to go, but he would see me off. I smiled. I knew God had other plans.

When we arrived at the train station, Gary had real strong doubts about going. However, when it came time to get on the train, Gary made the right decision. We were Cape Town bound.

Gary followed me onto the train, and he and I went into a first class department that was empty. Gary and I had that compartment to ourselves for half of twenty some hours that we were traveling. The other half of the trip, we shared the compartment with two Christian brothers.

When we arrived at Cape Town, Dave was there to meet us. Dave had information for me about an organization called Mfesane (this word means compassion in the Xhosa language). I found out later that their name came from Matthew 14:14.

And Jesus went forth, and saw a great multitude, and was moved with compassion toward them, and he healed their sick.

I called Mfesane and set up an appointment to meet the director at the airport on August 7th, 1997. On the way to Khayalitcha, Gary was acting very nervous, and Dave was very quiet. They both had good reasons. There was a policeman killed in Khayalitcha the night before, and a young woman named Amy was brutally attacked and murdered there. In addition, the bus driver was telling us not to go into Khayalitcha. We were informed that horrible murders had taken place there.

The director of Mfesane picked us up at the airport. I noticed a change right away. A change that I can't completely describe or explain. The two words that I believe best describes the experience are Holy Ghost. Dave, Gary and I had a peace and witnessed a presence of the power of God.

We started to act as one. It was clear that the Holy Spirit was operating through me and directed both Dave and Gary the whole time we were in Khayalitcha. All fear was absent and we set our minds to accomplish the task. However, none of us knew what that task was. Yet, are minds or maybe I should say "mind" seemed to know what questions to ask and how to respond to the answers.

To this day, I don't know why God sent three white males, who just met from three different countries, into Khayalitcha. I do know that an issue of prayer was addressed and that many people told us that no white man could go into Khayalicha and live. Also, I sent a report of my trip to a few people that I thought may help Mfesane. However, I don't know if anyone responded to the report.

Also, I do know and understand that I was so focused on going to Khayalitcha that I didn't dwell on hardships, inconveniences and dangers along the way. I ministered to others around me, and they received life changing experiences, as well as people were converted to Christianity.

I stayed ten more weeks in Cape Town. I worked with the local church helping the homeless, and many were helped and delivered from the kingdom of darkness and conveyed into the kingdom of light..

Chapter 7

I left Cape Town the day the revival started. I was going to go to Madagascar, but at the last moment I believed the Lord wanted me to go to Jerusalem. So, I purchased a ticket to Israel.

Once I arrived in Jerusalem, I went to the youth hostel. I just happened to be placed in a room with a pastor, missionary and Christian student. I asked them, "Why are you in Jerusalem"? They all let me know that they were there for an international Christian conference. So, I attended the conference with them.

Most of my time in Israel was a growth experience. However, I did do some witnessing, and three people received Jesus as their savior: two of them were Muslim and one was a German tourist.

The lord gave me a word of knowledge in Israel. I was to submit to the pastor that first baptized me when I was 12 years old. At the time of my baptism, he was the pastor of the Baptist church located in Davison, Michigan. But when I returned home, he was pastor of the Baptist church located in Burton, Michigan.

Church history
When I attended the Baptist church located in Davison, Michigan as a boy, my sisters and I liked

watching the church service from the balcony. However, one day during service I noticed an electronic devise, and I started examining it. While I was playing with it, something got unplugged or turned off. The result was the Sunday service was no longer being broadcasted on the radio.

Why am I bringing this up? Because when I met this pastor who I haven't seen for over twenty years, it was the first thing that he remembered about me. So much for first impressions!!!

However, God is greater than our mistakes. The pastor invited me to a church leadership meeting. At that meeting, I was put in charge of starting home cell groups and evangelism outreach.

The home cell groups started in my home and grew to several groups with the help of brother Ellis who took over the home cell groups. That's when I focused on the evangelism outreach on Saturdays and a mission trip to Northern Ireland, Ireland, and England.

Now, here comes "the truth about truth". If you know the truth, you put the needs and desires of others above your own needs and desires (1 John 3:16). If you don't know the truth, you follow your own selfish desires and ambitions (Romans 2:8).

People, even people who call themselves brothers and sisters in Christ, can have hidden agendas that will fight against God's plan. While one or more members in the church are working to build something, there can be one or more members in the same church working to tear it down. Especially, when they think they are the real leadership in the church and everything must meet with their approval.

These self-centered believers know how to use gossip like a sword. They are siding with the accuser of the brethren, and they are allowing Satan to manifest in their flesh. May God have mercy on them because they know not what they do. They are ignorant children who don't hear the voice of Love. This is what the Bible says about it:

Isaiah 58: 9-11 NIV
If you take away the yoke of oppression, with the pointing of the finger and malicious talk, and if you spend yourselves in behalf of the hungry and satisfy the needs of the oppressed, then your light will rise in darkness, and your night will become like the noonday. The Lord will guide you always; he will satisfy your needs in a sun-scorched land and will strengthen your frame. You will be like a well watered garden, like a spring whose waters will never fail.

Please hear my plea. If you are talking about anybody in a negative way, stop! Stop! Stop! Repent! Be a part of the solution and not a part of the problem.

The point is that the gossip and slandering was so bad in the church that people were telling my mother things about me that she knew for a fact weren't true. However, Satan knows that if you say something loud enough, long enough, that people will start questioning the truth.

Know this and understand: When you rise above where people think you ought to be, you will offend them; offended people will take action against you in some form (Mark 6:3; Matthew 13:57, 58). So when you hear your call from God, guard it with this knowledge. For people who call you brother or sister will eat away every bit of your desire to do what you are called to do if you let them. Again, be cautious and walk circumspectly when it comes to your calling from God.

Next, came Satan's aha! Weapon. This is where an unbeliever or misguided brother or sister in Christ will try to find something wrong with your speech and/or actions. What's worse is when they don't find something they have a tendency to make something up, so they have something to aha! With the other aha! people.

Psalms 35:21
Yea, they opened their mouth wide against me, [and] said, Aha, aha, our eye hath seen [it[.

Psalms 40:15
Let them be desolate for a reward of their shame that say unto me, Aha, aha.

Psalms 70:3
Let them be turned back for a reward of their shame that say, Aha, aha.

Please understand there were many wonderful brothers and sisters in the church who walked in the love of God. However, the scripture let's us know there are weeds among the wheat.

Matthew 13:24-30
24 Another parable put he forth unto them, saying, The kingdom of heaven is likened unto a man which sowed good seed in his field: 25 But while men slept, his enemy came and sowed tares among the wheat, and went his way. 26 But when the blade was sprung up, and brought forth fruit, then appeared the tares also. 27 So the servants of the householder came and said unto him, Sir, didst not thou sow good seed in thy field? from whence then hath it tares? 28 He said unto them,

An enemy hath done this. The servants said unto him, Wilt thou then that we go and gather them up? 29 But he said, Nay; lest while ye gather up the tares, ye root up also the wheat with them. 30 Let both grow together until the harvest: and in the time of harvest I will say to the reapers, Gather ye together first the tares, and bind them in bundles to burn them: but gather the wheat into my barn.

We must dwell with the weeds even when they are chocking us. However, we don't call a weed good and a wheat bad.

Isaiah 5:20
20 Woe unto them that call evil good, and good evil; that put darkness for light, and light for darkness; that put bitter for sweet, and sweet for bitter!

The problem is not with having weeds in the church. The problem comes when they dominate to the point that good becomes evil and evil becomes good.
Remember mercy triumphs over judgment. Love those who are not lovely. Help those who think they don't need help. Pray for those who despitefully use you. Run! When God says, "run". Stand! When God says, "stand". Fight! when God says, "fight".
Leave! When God says, "leave".
I believed it was time to leave, and I realized that strife in the church was a very bad thing. So, I prayed about my situation; the solution was go to a church that was nearby and submit to the pastor for Spiritual guidance. I ended up staying in that church while I ran mission trips into Central America and Canada.
Please pray this prayer with me:

Father, I thank you for my brothers and sisters, even the ones who gossip, point fingers and say, "Aha!." May your unconditional, unfailing, and perfect love flow through me and touch their hearts and souls. May I trust in you, keep my eyes on you, and not on them. Help me to be a witness to them and may your grace teach them to act in love. In Jesus name, Amen!

The Lens of God
When I was in Bible College, I learned that scripture interprets scripture. So, I was meditating on scripture when the thought came to me to use scripture as a lens to magnify other scripture.

Psalms 36:9 NIV
For with you is the fountain of life; in your light we see light.

Psalms 119:130 NIV
The unfolding of your word gives light; it gives understanding to the simple.

The word of God is God (John 1:1-14). God is love (1 John 4:8). Love has depth (Ephesians 3:18). Therefore, I'm comfortable in meditating on the word of God with the word of God, and I believe that this method of meditation gives me a deeper understanding of God's word.

Please don't build any religious ideas around this practice. I'm just showing you in my testimony a way that I meditate to get a deeper understanding of what God is saying to me through His word.

The lens I'm using is 2 Corinthians 10:3. The scripture that I'm looking at through the lens is James 1:1-2:26. The result is the following interpretation.

2 Corinthians 10:3
For though we walk in the flesh, we do not war after the flesh:

The following interpretation of James 1:1 – 2:26 may help you to soldier on when people who call themselves brothers and sisters become the biggest hindrance to your calling.

James reflected upon
(through the lens of 2 Corinthians 10:3)

Faith must be tested (1:1-4).

Tested faith over a long period of time develops a believers ability to stand and do what is necessary to finish the task. When a believer completes this process, he or she is complete in every way; the believer is able to carry on in the mission of destroying the works of the devil. In other words, the believer is a weapon (soldier) forged against the kingdom of darkness.

1:5
A good soldier knows that he must depend on his superiors to guide him into battle and explain his part in the battle. Without this wisdom an army can't fight as one. Therefore, every soldier must know his position and fight according to the weapons, abilities and strategies that he has been given.

1:6-8
When the soldier has received the plan from his commander, he must carry it out believing in the cause over personal safety and comfort. When a soldier starts focusing on his situation instead of the plan to

overcome the enemy unto victory, doubt can cause the soldier to divide his thoughts between two or more possibilities. This can effect his ability to hear future orders because he is unstable in all his ways.

1:9-12
Whatever the soldier's circumstance, he must focus his mind on the things that will gain victory. He must continue in the battle plan until the reward of victory is achieved.

1:13-21
The commanding officer is not the enemy nor does he act the way the enemy acts. So, do not blame your commander when your own thoughts and desires drag you into a deadly situation. The commander always has the best interest of his soldiers at heart while knowing that some must be scarified (which the commander has given us an example-the cross) in order to win the war.
Therefore, it is the enemy that leads you away from the main battle and will let you have fake victories that are insignificant. So, you must follow the commander's word (battle plan). In other words, trust your commander and get rid of any other opinion on the subject including yours.

1:22-27
Remember that receiving orders from your commander is not enough. You must act on those orders in order to achieve the desired result. It is very important to speak in line with the orders you receive so you don't get confused and/or open yourself to attack from the enemy. Make sure to help those you can help as you carry on in the battle.

2:1-13

Soldiers are part of a fighting unit and each member knows his place. Do not show favoritism but rather understand your position in Christ and follow those who are in leadership. If someone gets out of position because or their wealth or any other reason, they will exploit you and you will loose your effectiveness as a fighting unit.

You are soldiers of Christ and you are called to love. So, love others as you have been commanded to do so by our commander and general, King Jesus. Mercy is our weapon against judgment and you must overcome evil with good (Mat 5:44).

2:14-26

You know, it's not the man that talks a good fight that wins, but the man that actively fights the foe. Therefore, a good soldier has faith in his orders and fights the good fight of faith. He looks to the author and finisher of his faith and not at his circumstances.

James through 1 Timothy 4:4,5 NIV (lens)

For everything God created is good and nothing is to be rejected if it is received with thanksgiving, because it is consecrated by the word of God and prayer.

1:1-12

Every situation you face should be accepted for nothing is to be rejected. This includes various trials and tribulations. By accepting the situation and dealing with it through the word of God, prayer and being thankful in the face of all adversity, you grow up.

God accepts you when you ask Him for wisdom. He doesn't look at your good points or bad points to decide whether you should get wisdom or not. He accepts any who asks and he gives them wisdom.

However, you must have faith in order to receive. Even though God gives wisdom without exception, you can't receive it unless you believe.

Therefore, accept your situation for whatever situation you are in, it will soon pass away. You will persevere and receive a reward as long as you are thankful, prayerful and keep your mind on the word of God.

James through the lens of Hebrews 2:2

Looking unto Jesus the author and finisher of our faith; who for the joy that was set before him endured the cross, despising the shame, and is set down at the right hand of the throne of God.

1:1-12

Jesus wants His kingdom to know that He has given us an example of how to face difficult situations. He counted it all joy when he faced the trial of the cross. He persevered through every form of physical and mental cruelty and counted it all joy.

When Jesus was on the mount of olives, He asked the Father to take this cup from Him. He was seeking the Fathers wisdom for His upcoming trail. Whenever we are going through a trial we can seek the wisdom of our heavenly Father.

We can look to Him who is the author of our faith and He will help us receive the wisdom that He has given us who ask.

Whether you are rich or poor you need faith. Without it you will not stand the trial and you will wither away like the plant under the scorching sun.

James through the lens of John 7:5 (NIV)
For even his own brothers did not believe in him.

1:1

Know who you are in Christ when you address those who are called your brothers. Be firm in your identity even when others don't agree with it.

1:2-12

Count it joy when you are opposed by those who should love you. For Jesus Himself had brothers who didn't believe in Him. However, He knew His identity, and He persevered through their unbelief.

Jesus showed Himself wise in every situation so, we know that he lacked nothing and He wasn't double minded even though His brothers did not believe. Therefore, It is possible to overcome the wrong thinking of others - even those who are close to us.

Jesus became poor so that we could be rich. He is an example of how we should act in every financial situation. He stood the test and received His reward. We are able to receive this same state of mind through God's love for us.

1:13-15

When people close to us don't agree with us we can be tempted to doubt and fall into unbelief. However, if we focus on God and not our self-centeredness, we can stay away from that slippery slope. Also, it's easy to take offense and be unforgiving when someone close to you does not see things the way that you do.

1:16-18

Do not look to your brothers who don't believe God's call upon your life and don't be deceived by their ignorance and lack of faith. For what is good comes from above and the Father gives freely to those who believe. Whether your brothers believe in you or not.

1:16-27

Watch what you say around those who don't believe who God says you are. People take offense when someone doesn't fit into the mold that they think the person should fit into and they can become angry.

Accept what God has to say. Keep it hidden in your heart. Speak what God has planted in you and act upon it in faith.

If you don't do these things, what you know from God will fade away. You are either molded by hearing, speaking and acting on what God says or by those who are opposing what God says. <u>Who you really are in Christ will fade away if you listen to those who do not believe what God says about you</u>.

Therefore, watch what you say and who you say it to, as well as help those who need help. Don't pollute yourself with the unbelief and doubt of others.

Chapter 8

During my missionary travels, I developed what I call Guesthouse ministry. I would go to a guesthouse in a target country, and minister to people as they would come and go.

I would choose guesthouses that were known to have had many international travelers. This way I could set in one spot and evangelize people from all over the world.

My favorite spot for Guesthouse ministry was the youth hostel in Halifax, Nova Scotia. It was while I was on a mission trip there in Canada, I saw a newspaper advertisement. It read, "Teach English in South Korea".

I went to a lecture at Dalhousie University with a new believer. After, I heard the lecture; I knew that this was my new course of direction.

I needed a bachelor's degree in order to qualify for employment as a teacher in South Korea. So, when I finished my mission trip, I went back to Michigan. Next, I transferred my transcripts from the University of Michigan to Baker College. There was an accelerated learning program at Baker College that would allow me to graduate in less than a year and a half with my transferred credits.

After my first semester at Baker College, I started a club with several other students. The idea of the club was to go through our university program as a team. The club was called the "Synergy Club." In case you don't know what synergy means: It's when people work together they can accomplish more than they could as individuals. The members of synergy club worked together to help each other obtain high grade point averages and to make the learning process more comfortable and enjoyable.

This process started with finding out everything about the college program that we were planning on completing. We researched the courses that we were going to take before we took them and we gathered information on each professor's teaching style and how we could prepare for each course before it started. This way there was little to no surprises in the classroom, and we had advanced warnings on most class activities. In addition, the facts that we gathered helped us to determine the best professor for the course that we were taking and securing a place in that professor's class.

The end result was that everyone in the club received higher grade point averages than they ever had in their lives. Also, the learning materials were easier to comprehend and the classes were more beneficial and fun.

Therefore, there were great advantages for those of us who participated in the synergy club group, and members saw the completion of many tasks and the solving of many problems. The synergy that was produced in our group effort was greater than any individual effort. In other words, by working in our group an individual learned easier and faster than he or she could have learned on their own. According to the Holy

Bible (NIV) "Two are better than one, because they have a good return for their work: If one falls down, his friend can help him up (Ecc. 4:9-10).

How does the group work?

Learners work together building a community atmosphere in which all members feel free to give their points of view and do their part. Each member of the group can contribute to the group rules and help determine the goals and learning strategies for the group. Each member of the group has strengths and weaknesses and group members who are stronger in one area can help those members who are weaker in that area. Therefore, everyone in the group has a part to fulfill and anyone of the group members could be a teacher or mentor one moment and a student the next moment. If something comes up that requires additional help, we can seek outside help when needed

You may have asked yourself, "what does this have to do with anything?"

The whole point of this part of my testimony is to help you see the importance of the cell church. You put God, spirit-filled believers and the Holy Bible at the center of this group and you have church and an evangelistic outreach that encourages one another to succeed.

In the Bible, the cell church, home cell group or house church is mentioned. There were two types of meetings in the early church. Disciples gathered at the temple and they also met in their homes (Acts 2:46, 47). By Acts 8, the disciples have delegated authority to preach and minister to the needs of the people. These house churches developed leaders who are mentioned in Acts 16:40, Romans 16:3-5 & Philemon 2).

According to Ephesians 4:11 (NIV), "It was he who gave some to be apostles, some to be prophets, some to be evangelists, and some to be pastors and teachers to prepare God's people for works of service, so that the body of Christ may be built up."

The five fold ministry is the leadership structure that God has ordained for fellowship. The purpose of apostles, prophets, evangelists, pastors, and teachers is to:

1. Make known the Gospel
2. Establish and build churches
3. Point saints into relationship with God
4. Trouble shoot: deal with problems inside and outside the church
5. Be a physical example of the Father's love
6. Edify the body of believers
7. Equip the body of believers

Thus, the cell church is a family unit used to minister to individual needs and a place of discipleship. Also, it's a place to learn leadership and develop five fold ministry skills, as well as a loving environment that encourages growth in Christ.

Conclusion

I arranged my testimony and corresponding teachings and information in this book to help you understand who the real God is and the importance of fellowshipping with him.

Then, I tried to show you that God has called everyone to do something and that includes you. So, it is important to recognize what God has called you to do.

Next, I placed information and teaching in this book to help equip you for your calling, as well as give testimony to encourage you into fellowship with God and each other and give you experiential knowledge of how God can work through someone who is in relationship with Him. In addition, I enclosed individual teachings on witnessing and evangelism, as well as discipleship, church relationships, prayer, and praise.

Finally, I hoped my testimony revealed that God can use imperfect people to carry out His perfect plan. Therefore, everyone can participate in God's plan and answer His call. Also, I'm concluding my book with some Good advice and an encouraging word to help you move forward in what God has called you to do.

Good Advice
1. Don't walk when you need to run.

1 Corinthians 9:24-27 (NIV)
Do you not know that in a race all the runners run, but only one gets the prize? Run in such a way as to get the prize. [25] Everyone who competes in the games goes into strict training. They do it to get a crown that will not last; but we do it to get a crown that will last forever. [26] Therefore I do not run like a man running aimlessly; I do not fight like a man beating the air. [27] No, I beat my body and make it my slave so that after I have preached to others, I myself will not be disqualified for the prize.

Galatians 2:2 (NIV)
I went in response to a revelation and set before them the gospel that I preach among the Gentiles. But I did this privately to those who seemed to be leaders, for fear that I was running or had run my race in vain.

Galatians 5:7-8 (NIV)
You were running a good race. Who cut in on you and kept you from obeying the truth? [8] That kind of persuasion does not come from the one who calls you.

Philippians 2:16 (NIV)
as you hold out the word of life—-in order that I may boast on the day of Christ that I did not run or labor for nothing.

Hebrews 12:1-3 (NIV)
Therefore, since we are surrounded by such a great cloud of witnesses, let us throw off everything that hinders and the sin that so easily entangles, and let us

run with perseverance the race marked out for us. [2] Let us fix our eyes on Jesus, the author and perfecter of our faith, who for the joy set before him endured the cross, scorning its shame, and sat down at the right hand of the throne of God. [3] Consider him who endured such opposition from sinful men, so that you will not grow weary and lose heart.

2 John 1:8-9 (NIV)
Watch out that you do not lose what you have worked for, but that you may be rewarded fully. [9] Anyone who runs ahead and does not continue in the teaching of Christ does not have God; whoever continues in the teaching has both the Father and the Son.

2. Know who you are in Christ.

2 Corinthians 5:17
Old things have passed away-I'm a new man

Ephesians 2:10-22
I was created a new man

1 Corinthians 15
How the new man was created. The resurrection - a seed sown in honor

Ephesians 3:14-20
You need to be rooted and grounded in love.

Ephesians 4
The new man knows where he fits in The unity of the body of Christ, walks in unity, is taught by God & doesn't grieve the Holy Spirit.

Ephesians 5
Walk in love, light, wisdom & submission

Colossians 3:1-17
Character of the new man

Galatians 3:26-29
You are under the blessing

Psalms 112
Description of you walking in the blessing

Ephesians 2:6
You are alive with Christ and sit in heavenly places

Romans 8:10
You are dead to sin and alive to righteousness

Galatians 3:27
Put on the new man

2 Timothy 1:7
You have a spirit of power, love and a sound mind

Ephesians 4:29
Be careful in speech

Galatians 6:9-10 (NIV)
Do good to all and do not grow weary and loose heart because he knows he'll reap in due season.

2 Corinthians 4:2
Renounce secrete and shameful ways; do not use deception nor distort the word of God.

Ephesians 4:29
Encourage and edify

Romans 1:28-32
Description of the old nature

Romans 8:28
The change happens in the heart

Proverbs 23:7
As you think in your heart, so are you.

Romans 10:9-10
You believe from your heart and speak with your mouth (Mat.15:19, Mk. 7:21 & Lu 6:45).

Ephesians 4:23 & Romans 12:2
Renew your mind

2 Timothy 3:15
The Holy Scriptures are able to make you wise

Hebrews 4:12
The word of God is living and active

1 Corinthians 15:1-4
Christ died for our sins and was resurrected on the 3rd day.

1 Corinthians 15:21-22; 45-49
Death came through one man-resurrection came through one man

Called

Romans 6:4-14 & Galatians 5:24-25
The old man was crucified with Christ and we are alive to God

Romans 8:1-17
Law of the spirit of life

Ephesians 2
Made alive and one in Christ

1 Corinthians 15:35-58
Resurrected body

James 1:21
The implanted word is able to save your soul

James 1:22-25
Be doers of the word

1 Thessalonians 3:5
You are three parts

Ephesians 3:15
You have his name

Ephesians 3:16
You receive from God by your inner man

Ephesians 3:17
God dwells in your heart through faith

Ephesians 3:18
Relationship with God will ground us and give us roots

Ephesians 3:19 & 1 Corinthians 8:1
Love surpasses knowledge

Ephesians 3:20
God works through you

1 John 2:5
Keeping God's word perfects love

1 John 4:12
Loving one another in Christ perfects God's love in us.

1 John 4:16
God is love, and you who abide in love abide in God

1 John 4:17
Love is perfected in the confidence that we are like God in this world.

Romans 5:5
The love of God is poured out in your heart by the Holy Ghost

Jude 1:20-21
Pray in the Holy Spirit to build yourself up in your most holy faith and keep yourself in God's love

1 John 3:17
You share with your brother if you are abiding in love

Galatians 5:13-14
Faith works only through love

1 Corinthians 13:1-2
You're nothing without love

Romans 8:28 (NIV)
And we know that in all things God works for the good of those who love him, who have been called according to his purpose.

Romans 8:37 (NIV)
No, in all these things we are more than conquerors through him who loved us.

Hebrews 10:24 & Matthew 24:12
Stir up love

1 Timothy 1:5
The purpose of the love commandment

Ephesians 4:15-16
Speak the truth in love and do your part (Ephesians 4:1-16)

Ephesians 5:8
Walk as children in the light

Ephesians 5:13-15
Christ will give you light

Philippians 2:15
You are light in the world

Colossians 1:12
The Father qualified us to be children of light

1 Thessalonians 5:5
You are a son of the light

James 1:7
The Father of lights gives gifts

1 Peter 2:9
we are a chosen generation

1 John 1:7
If we walk in the light, we have fellowship with one another

John 12:36
Believe in the light so you can become sons of the light

James 1:18-22 & James 2:20-24
The word of God planted in us and acted upon produces children of the light

Hebrews 6:12
Faith + patience = success and victory

1 Corinthians 2:10-16
You are able to know and speak spiritual things through the spirit of God

Ephesians 1:3-14
How you receive Christ

Ephesians 5:6
Let no one deceive you with empty words

Ephesians 6:17
The word of God is our sword

Colossians 3:16
Let the word of God dwell in you

1 Thessalonians 2:13
The word of God is at work in believers

2 Timothy 2:15
A good worker correctly handles the word of truth

Hebrews 4:12
The word of God is living and active

1 Peter 1:23
You are born of the word of God (seed)

1John 2:5
Obey the word of God and walk as Jesus did

3. Don't do yourself harm

Matthew 4:4 & Hosea 4:6
What you don't know can cause you harm

Matthew 15:10-20
It's what comes out of a man's mouth that defiles a man (Matthew 12:34)

Matthew 12:37
Your words help you or hurt you

Proverbs 4:23 (NIV)
Above all else, guard your heart, for it is the wellspring of life.

Philippians 4:4-9
Worrying, not praying, not rejoicing, not guarding your heart and mind with God's peace, not being thankful,

and not following those God placed over us can lead to harm

Job 3:25
Don't be afraid or you can draw destruction upon yourself

James 3:16 & Romans 6:23
Strife and other sins open the door for the enemy to attack you

Numbers 14: 26-35
Grumbling and complaining kill God's promise and blessing

Proverbs 1:32
Complacency, self-satisfaction especially when accompanied by unawareness of actual dangers or deficiencies, is a destroyer.

4. Give yourself credit when credit is due.

1 Samuel 17:32-37 (NIV)
David said to Saul, "Let no one lose heart on account of this Philistine; your servant will go and fight him." [33] Saul replied, "You are not able to go out against this Philistine and fight him; you are only a boy, and he has been a fighting man from his youth." [34] But David said to Saul, "Your servant has been keeping his father's sheep. When a lion or a bear came and carried off a sheep from the flock, [35] I went after it, struck it and rescued the sheep from its mouth. When it turned on me, I seized it by its hair, struck it and killed it. [36] Your servant has killed both the lion and the bear; this uncircumcised Philistine will be like one of

them, because he has defied the armies of the living God. [37] The Lord who delivered me from the paw of the lion and the paw of the bear will deliver me from the hand of this Philistine." Saul said to David, "Go, and the Lord be with you."

1 Corinthians 9:27 (NIV)
No, I beat my body and make it my slave so that after I have preached to others, I myself will not be disqualified for the prize.

Philippians 4:10-13 (NIV)
I rejoice greatly in the Lord that at last you have renewed your concern for me. Indeed, you have been concerned, but you had no opportunity to show it. [11] I am not saying this because I am in need, for I have learned to be content whatever the circumstances. [12] I know what it is to be in need, and I know what it is to have plenty. I have learned the secret of being content in any and every situation, whether well fed or hungry, whether living in plenty or in want. [13] I can do everything through him who gives me strength.

5. Be like Jesus Christ and destroy the works of the devil

1 John 3:8
8 He that committeth sin is of the devil; for the devil sinneth from the beginning. For this purpose the Son of God was manifested, that he might destroy the works of the devil.

Acts 10:38 (NIV)
how God anointed Jesus of Nazareth with the Holy Spirit and power, and how he went around doing good

and healing all who were under the power of the devil, because God was with him.

Romans 13:12
12 The night is far spent, the day is at hand: let us therefore cast off the works of darkness, and let us put on the armour of light.

6. Give until it hurts

Mark 12:41-43
41 And Jesus sat over against the treasury, and beheld how the people cast money into the treasury: and many that were rich cast in much. 42 And there came a certain poor widow, and she threw in two mites, which make a farthing. 43 And he called[unto him] his disciples, and saith unto them, Verily I say unto you, That this poor widow hath cast more in, than all they which have cast into the treasury:

Matthew 5:42 (NIV)
Give to the one who asks you, and do not turn away from the one who wants to borrow from you.

Luke 6:38 (NIV)
Give, and it will be given to you. A good measure, pressed down, shaken together and running over, will be poured into your lap. For with the measure you use, it will be measured to you."

7. Do what God tells you to do

1 Samuel 15:22
22 And Samuel said, Hath the Lord[as great] delight in burnt offerings and sacrifices, as in obeying the voice

of the LORD? Behold, to obey[is] better than sacrifice,[and] to hearken than the fat of rams.

Matthew 7:21-24
21 Not every one that saith unto me, Lord, Lord, shall enter into the kingdom of heaven; but he that doeth the will of my Father which is in heaven. 22 Many will say to me in that day, Lord, Lord, have we not prophesied in thy name? and in thy name have cast out devils? and in thy name done many wonderful works? 23 And then will I profess unto them, I never knew you: depart from me, ye that work iniquity. 24 Therefore whosoever heareth these sayings of mine, and doeth them, I will liken him unto a wise man, which built his house upon a rock:

James 1:22
22 But be ye doers of the word, and not hearers only, deceiving your own selves.

Closing Encouragement & Edification

The people of Israel fell away from God and would not listen to His instruction. It's important to understand the symptoms so, if you are experiencing them, you can repent and get back into fellowship with God. You need to be in fellowship with God in order to hear, understand and have the wisdom to do what God has called you to do.

Jeremiah 8
V4: The Lord tells us that it's normal when a man falls for him to get up or if he turns away for him to return.

Jeremiah 7 (NIV):
[22] For when I brought your ancestors out of Egypt and spoke to them, I did not just give them commands about burnt offerings and sacrifices, [23] but I gave them this command: Obey me, and I will be your God and you will be my people. Walk in obedience to all I command you, that it may go well with you. [24] But they did not listen or pay attention; instead, they followed the stubborn inclinations of their evil hearts. They went backward and not forward. [25] From the time your ancestors left Egypt until now, day after day, again and again I sent you my servants the prophets. [26] But they did not listen to me or pay attention. They were stiff-necked and did more evil than their ancestors.'

[27] "When you tell them all this, they will not listen to you; when you call to them, they will not answer. [28] Therefore say to them, 'This is the nation that has not obeyed the LORD its God or responded to correction. Truth has perished; it has vanished from their lips.

Your heart condition is very important. If your heart is not right, you either won't know what your calling is, or you are hearing and acting on what you think your calling is based on sensual knowledge. The people in these above verses all thought they were doing what they were called to do, but they were listening to their evil hearts and not to God (Jeremiah 7:24; Romans 1:28).

Romans 1 (NIV):
[18] The wrath of God is being revealed from heaven against all the godlessness and wickedness of men, who suppress the truth by their wickedness,

¹⁹ since what may be known about God is plain to them, because God has made it plain to them. ²⁰ For since the creation of the world God's invisible qualities—his eternal power and divine nature—have been clearly seen, being understood from what has been made, so that people are without excuse.

²¹ For although they knew God, they neither glorified him as God nor gave thanks to him, but their thinking became futile and their foolish hearts were darkened. ²² Although they claimed to be wise, they became fools ²³ and exchanged the glory of the immortal God for images made to look like a mortal human being and birds and animals and reptiles.

²⁴ Therefore God gave them over in the sinful desires of their hearts to sexual impurity for the degrading of their bodies with one another. ²⁵ They exchanged the truth about God for a lie, and worshiped and served created things rather than the Creator—who is forever praised. Amen.

²⁶ Because of this, God gave them over to shameful lusts. Even their women exchanged natural sexual relations for unnatural ones. ²⁷ In the same way the men also abandoned natural relations with women and were inflamed with lust for one another. Men committed shameful acts with other men, and received in themselves the due penalty for their error.

²⁸ Furthermore, just as they did not think it worthwhile to retain the knowledge of God, so God gave

them over to a depraved mind, so that they do what ought not to be done. [29] They have become filled with every kind of wickedness, evil, greed and depravity. They are full of envy, murder, strife, deceit and malice. They are gossips, [30] slanderers, God-haters, insolent, arrogant and boastful; they invent ways of doing evil; they disobey their parents; [31] they have no understanding, no fidelity, no love, no mercy. [32] Although they know God's righteous decree that those who do such things deserve death, they not only continue to do these very things but also approve of those who practice them.

V5: So why when Jerusalem (God's people) turned away they refuse to return.

Psalms 81 (NIV):
[10] I am the LORD your God,
who brought you up out of Egypt.
Open wide your mouth and I will fill it.
[11] "But my people would not listen to me;
Israel would not submit to me.
[12] So I gave them over to their stubborn hearts
to follow their own devices.
[13] "If my people would only listen to me,
if Israel would only follow my ways,
[14] how quickly I would subdue their enemies
and turn my hand against their foes!
[15] Those who hate the LORD would cringe before him,
and their punishment would last forever.
[16] But you would be fed with the finest of wheat;
with honey from the rock I would satisfy you."

Again, know your heart condition. What comes out of your mouth will reveal your heart condition (Matthew 15:17-20).

V8 They (God's people) think they are wise because they have the law, but handle it incorrectly.

John 5 (NIV):
[39] You diligently study the Scriptures because you think that in them you possess eternal life. These are the Scriptures that testify about me, [40] yet you refuse to come to me to have life.

What you need to know here is that scripture alone can't give you the answers. You have to have a relationship with the living God. This means that you need God's Holy Spirit living on the inside of you, and you need to be in fellowship with him in order to know the truth (John 16:13).

V9 To the point, they have rejected God's word. So, their wisdom is worldly.

James 3 (NIV):
[13] Who is wise and understanding among you? Let them show it by their good life, by deeds done in the humility that comes from wisdom. [14] But if you harbor bitter envy and selfish ambition in your hearts, do not boast about it or deny the truth. [15] Such "wisdom" does not come down from heaven but is earthly, unspiritual, demonic. [16] For where you have envy and selfish ambition, there you find disorder and every evil practice.

¹⁷ But the wisdom that comes from heaven is first of all pure; then peace-loving, considerate, submissive, full of mercy and good fruit, impartial and sincere. ¹⁸ Peacemakers who sow in peace reap a harvest of righteousness.

This scripture is giving you a mirror to look at to check your heart condition. Also, you are being told what happens when you reject God's word: You become worldly and act on human wisdom instead of Godly wisdom. Of course, this will affect your ability to understand your true calling.

V10 Therefore, they are under a curse.

> Galatians 3 (NIV):
> ¹⁰ For all who rely on the works of the law are under a curse, for it is written: "Cursed is everyone who does not continue to do everything written in the Book of the Law." ¹¹ Clearly no one who relies on the law is justified before God, because "the righteous will live by faith." ¹² The law is not based on faith; on the contrary, it says, "The person who does these things will live by them." ¹³ Christ redeemed us from the curse of the law by becoming a curse for us, for it is written: "Cursed is everyone who is hung on a pole." ¹⁴ He redeemed us in order that the blessing given to Abraham might come to the Gentiles through Christ Jesus, so that by faith we might receive the promise of the Spirit.

You must be a born-again, spirit-filled believer in order to hear and know God's call upon your life. This means you are in relationship with God and following Him and not the rules (2 Titus 2:11-14).

V11 They make peace where there is no peace.

> Psalms 120 (NIV):
> [7] I am for peace;
> but when I speak, they are for war.

When a born-again believer speaks, there is going to be a fight. It's not that you want a fight or you are asking for a fight – it's because you are not of this world and this world rejects you (1 John 3:12, 13). If you are not fighting the enemy, perhaps you are walking the same way (Amos 3:3).

V 12 Their conscience is seared with a hot iron.

> 1 Timothy 4 (NIV):
> [1] The Spirit clearly says that in later times some will abandon the faith and follow deceiving spirits and things taught by demons. [2] Such teachings come through hypocritical liars, whose consciences have been seared as with a hot iron. [3] They forbid people to marry and order them to abstain from certain foods, which God created to be received with thanksgiving by those who believe and who know the truth. [4] For everything God created is good, and nothing is to be rejected if it is received with thanksgiving, [5] because it is consecrated by the word of God and prayer.

Notice how your conscience is seared. Your conscience is seared by following demons that forbid certain activities and things. This is the same as worldly religious practice and what men do when they don't want to follow God's will and call. When Judas didn't want to follow the ways of Jesus, he ran to the religious people of his time to find the help he needed to get what he wanted (Luke 22:4). However, knowing the end of the story, Judas didn't get what he wanted and he died at his own hand (Relationship with God = life and worldly religion = death).

V 13 Their wealth is laid up for the just.

> Proverbs 13:22 (NIV)
> [22] A good person leaves an inheritance for their children's children, but a sinner's wealth is stored up for the righteous.

Rejoice! You have the resources you need to do what God is called you to do.

V14 They are running away from responsibility.

> Romans 15 (NIV):
> [16] to be a minister of Christ Jesus to the Gentiles with the priestly duty of proclaiming the gospel of God, so that the Gentiles might become an offering acceptable to God, sanctified by the Holy Spirit.

God has given us a great responsibility. We are to spread the Gospel of Jesus Christ. Whatever you are called to do, we all have this responsibility.

V15 Their dreams are not coming true.

> Jeremiah 23 (NIV):
> [32] Indeed, I am against those who prophesy false dreams," declares the LORD. "They tell them and lead my people astray with their reckless lies, yet I did not send or appoint them. They do not benefit these people in the least," declares the LORD.

If your calling is from God, it will come to pass. So, do not confuse a false calling or dream with waiting on God. It is a common mistake for Christians to give up before their dreams come to pass. However, if they don't come to pass in a reasonable amount of time, it may be an indication that your calling is false, and you should seek council from church leadership if you have any doubts.

V16 the enemy is attacking from without,

> 1 Peter 5 (NIV):
> [8] Be self-controlled and alert. Your enemy the devil prowls around like a roaring lion looking for someone to devour. [9] Resist him, standing firm in the faith, because you know that your brothers throughout the world are undergoing the same kind of sufferings.

Again, you are reminded that there is no peace. The enemy must be resisted. You can't resist the enemy if you are ignorant. You must know who you are and where you are going. When you move toward your vision there should be some kind of resistance. You must fight the good fight of faith to overcome the devil's resistance to God's call upon your life.

V17 and the enemy is attacking from within.

> Ephesians 2:1- 5 (NIV):
> [1] As for you, you were dead in your transgressions and sins, [2] in which you used to live when you followed the ways of this world and of the ruler of the kingdom of the air, the spirit who is now at work in those who are disobedient. [3] All of us also lived among them at one time, gratifying the cravings of our flesh[a] and following its desires and thoughts. Like the rest, we were by nature deserving of wrath. [4] But because of his great love for us, God, who is rich in mercy, [5] made us alive with Christ even when we were dead in transgressions—it is by grace you have been saved.

If you don't have God's Holy Spirit, you can't follow him. You can't follow what you don't have. If you are saved, you should have an inward witness to that fact. If you aren't saved and don't have the inward witness, you need to establish this before proceeding to what you are called to do. Once you have this inward guarantee, you know that you know that you know you are saved, then understand God gives you the grace to accomplish everything you need to do (Titus 2:11-14).

V18 The Holy Spirit is grieved.

> Ephesians 4 (NIV):
> [29] Do not let any unwholesome talk come out of your mouths, but only what is helpful for building others up according to their needs, that it may benefit those who listen. [30] And do not grieve the Holy Spirit of God, with whom you were sealed for

the day of redemption. [31] Get rid of all bitterness, rage and anger, brawling and slander, along with every form of malice. [32] Be kind and compassionate to one another, forgiving each other, just as in Christ God forgave you.

You get what you say. Therefore, watch what you say. Wrong speech can effect your calling.

V19-22   His people are cursed. This resulted in the fact that they would not return (Jeremiah 8:4)

If you heard God's call and didn't respond, you have hardened your heart. During this hardening process you heard God less and less. The good news is that you can repent and reverse this process. The Bible clearly tells you in Jeremiah 8 and through other scriptures that God desires that you hear and obey His voice. If you do fall down and turn away, He expects you to get up and start doing what He asked you to do.
Also, the Holy Scriptures are full of examples of how people have hindrances and darkness in their lives and God gave them light, the word of truth, and victory over their circumstance or situation was obtained.

Matthew 9:1-8 (NIV)
Jesus stepped into a boat, crossed over and came to his own town. [2] Some men brought to him a paralytic, lying on a mat. When Jesus saw their faith, he said to the paralytic, "Take heart, son; your sins are forgiven." [3] At this, some of the teachers of the law said to themselves, "This fellow is blaspheming!" [4] Knowing their thoughts, Jesus said, "Why do you entertain evil thoughts in your hearts? [5] Which is easier: to say,

'Your sins are forgiven,' or to say, 'Get up and walk'? [6] But so that you may know that the Son of Man has authority on earth to forgive sins" Then he said to the paralytic, "Get up, take your mat and go home." [7] And the man got up and went home. [8] When the crowd saw this, they were filled with awe; and they praised God, who had given such authority to men.

There are at least two situations being dealt with in these verses. First, there is a paralytic who had people carrying him. His situation was that he was paralyzed physically, but these people were acting in faith. They supported the handicapped person and he received the command to get up and the paralytic overcame the hindrance through obedience to the Lord's word.

Second, the religious people were paralyzed by their evil thinking and the lord shed His light on their darkness and many people caught the revelation, because one man with faith followed the Lord's command and got up.

When you are in the dark about something and/or are being hindered because of life's circumstances, listen for the Lord's instruction, get up and do what he tells you. He might just set others free in the process.

Isaiah 60:1-3 (NIV)
"Arise, shine, for your light has come, and the glory of the Lord rises upon you. [2] See, darkness covers the earth and thick darkness is over the peoples, but the Lord rises upon you and his glory appears over you. [3] Nations will come to your light, and kings to the brightness of your dawn.

When you hear the call of the Lord and act in obedience, you become a bright light that draws people to you. Because people are in dark places, and they long for the light that frees their souls.

Also, sometimes the light meets people who are in dark places on the road they are traveling on. In any case He still gives His instruction and those who get up and do what the Lord commands will see results.

Acts 9:1-6 (NIV)
Meanwhile, Saul was still breathing out murderous threats against the Lord's disciples. He went to the high priest [2] and asked him for letters to the synagogues in Damascus, so that if he found any there who belonged to the Way, whether men or women, he might take them as prisoners to Jerusalem. [3] As he neared Damascus on his journey, suddenly a light from heaven flashed around him. [4] He fell to the ground and heard a voice say to him, "Saul, Saul, why do you persecute me?" [5] "Who are you, Lord?" Saul asked. "I am Jesus, whom you are persecuting," he replied. [6] "Now get up and go into the city, and you will be told what you must do."

It's obvious that God doesn't need our help to reveal Himself to anybody. He did a great job of revealing Himself to Saul on His own. However, God has given us the privilege of spreading His gospel of peace. Therefore, acquire the understanding and rejoice in what you are called to do.

Acts 12:5-7 (NIV)
So Peter was kept in prison, but the church was earnestly praying to God for him. [6] The night before Herod was to bring him to trial, Peter was sleeping between two soldiers, bound with two chains, and sentries stood guard at the entrance. [7] Suddenly an angel of the Lord appeared and a light shone in the cell. He struck

Peter on the side and woke him up. "Quick, get up!" he said, and the chains fell off Peter's wrists.

    This scripture shows how people can be delivered by the prayers of saints. However, the saint that received the benefit of that prayer received a command from the Lord (v11), by an angel, to get up and do something. Peter got up and followed the instructions. The result was the unbelievable (Acts 12:8-16).

    What is the Lord calling you to do today? Did you get up and do what he told you to do? Was the result the unbelievable?

    Here are more examples:

Luke 6:8 (NIV)
But Jesus knew what they were thinking and said to the man with the shriveled hand, "Get up and stand in front of everyone." So he got up and stood there.

Luke 7:12-15 (NIV)
As he approached the town gate, a dead person was being carried out—-the only son of his mother, and she was a widow. And a large crowd from the town was with her. [13] When the Lord saw her, his heart went out to her and he said, "Don't cry." [14] Then he went up and touched the coffin, and those carrying it stood still. He said, "Young man, I say to you, get up!" [15] The dead man sat up and began to talk, and Jesus gave him back to his mother.

Judges 7:9 (NIV)
During that night the Lord said to Gideon, "Get up, go down against the camp, because I am going to give it into your hands.

Here's what happens if you hear the Lord's command and don't respond appropriately.

Luke 22:45-46 (NIV)
When he rose from prayer and went back to the disciples, he found them asleep, exhausted from sorrow. [46] "Why are you sleeping?" he asked them. "Get up and pray so that you will not fall into temptation."

If you've read the Bible, you know the rest of the story. Everyone of them went back to sleep and later they fell into temptation.

Are you sleeping when you should be praying? Are you holding back like the horse on the cover of this book?

There is a very real adversary that wants you to fail. He doesn't want you to get up.

Psalm 41:7-8 (NIV)
All my enemies whisper together against me; they imagine the worst for me, saying, [8] "A vile disease has beset him; he will never get up from the place where he lies."

However, we have a merciful God who helps us to get up when we ask Him. He not only helps us to get up, he helps us to be victorious over the enemy.

Psalm 41:10-11 (NIV)
But you, O Lord, have mercy on me; raise me up, that I may repay them. [11] I know that you are pleased with me, for my enemy does not triumph over me.

I hope these scriptures help you to get up. Once you get up you need to do what God has told you to do. Just get up and do it!

Do it!

There comes a time in everyone's life when they need to face the truth. Just like Pontus Pilot, who was face to face with the truth (Jesus), when he said, "What is truth?" So, I ask you, "Are you looking truth in the eyes today and not seeing that He's real?" Are you hearing His call? Are you getting up and doing it?

Reflect!

Prayer notes

We are called to intercede for one another. We are not called to accuse one another. If we are given a word of correction for someone, the Lord has a procedure to follow.

First, we seek Him in prayer. We ask Him to remove the plank in our own eye, and we listen for the still small voice of the Holy Spirit.

Second, we follow His instructions. If He doesn't give us any instructions, it's not a problem that we are to deal with at this time. Let it go! Trust God and move on. If you are given instructions, be obedient and follow them.

Third, stand, knowing God has a way of holding us together in the worst of times.

Fourth, we have a procedure for confrontation in the Bible (Matthew 18:15-17):

1. Go to the person or persons and talk about the situation you need to discuss.
2. If you didn't achieve or receive a satisfactory result, then take one or two witnesses with you.
3. If you didn't achieve or receive a satisfactory result, bring the person or persons in front of the church.

4. Understand that this process requires constant prayer and a willingness to love the people involved. Also, you should understand that the decision of others may not be in your favor, so rejoice whatever the outcome may be and accept the decision of the church.

When you follow the directions of the Holy Spirit every conflict will be an opportunity for promotion. The Lord gives us our greatest victories in the midst of impossible odds.

Through prayer we can grow in relationship with the Holy Spirit and He can answer our "who, what, where, when, why and how" questions. Prayer can help us to receive truth and discern truth, as well as overcome whatever trial we are facing including the forgiveness of people who hurt us and betray us. Let us move forward in relationship and do not look back. Lot's wife looked back and turned to salt. Go forward!

When we are in fellowship, God empowers our prayers. He helps us to discern what type of prayer we should use and how to apply the prayer in the situation we are praying for in order to be victorious.

Prayerlessness is a sin (1 Samuel 12:23).

I. Why do we pray?
   1. Communion with God (Matthew 6:6-8)
   2. reveals you to you (Isaiah 6:5)
   3. power to cleanse your heart from sin (Psalms 19:12, 13)
   4. power to hold us up (Psalms 17:5)
   5. power to govern our tongue (Psalms 141:3)
   6. power to open our eyes (Psalms 119:18)
   7. power to bring wisdom (James 1:5)

       8. power to bring Holy Spirit (Acts 1:14 & 2:4)
       9. power to bring salvation to others (1 John 5:16)
      10. power to forgive others (Matthew 6:14, 15)

II. How to pray
    a. Model prayers (Matthew 6:5-15 & 1 Chronicles 29:10-15)
    b. Ask: Pray out loud (James 4:2, Genesis 1:26-28 & Luke 11:9, 10)
    c. Pray God's will
       1. Don't ask amiss   James 4:3
       2. Submit to God   James 4:7
       3. Know His will   Colossians 1:9
       4. How you ask   1 John 5:14

1. Faith
    a. Ask in faith without doubting   Hebrews 11:1
    b. Prayer of faith can heal   James 1:6
    c. Faith = victory   James 5:15
    d. Three kinds of faith
       1. Measure of faith   Romans 12:3
       2. Faith by hearing   Romans 10:17
       3. Gift of faith   1 Corinthians 12:9
       4. Persistence
       Receiving because of persistence   Luke 11:8
       Persistent widow   Luke 18:1-8

5. Hope
    a. Natural expectation   Acts 27:20
    b. Sinful expectation   Acts 24:26
    c. Impossible   Romans 4:18
    d. Spiritual assurance   2 Corinthians 1:7

e. See the invisible	2 Corinthians 4:18
f. Manifests things	Romans 4:13-19
g. Immoveable hope	2 Corinthians 1:7
h. Living hope	1 Peter 1:3
i. Wait in hope	Romans 8:24-26

- NOTE: If you see it, you are in faith. If you don't see it, stand in hope until you do.

6. Stand
a. With armor	Ephesians 6:10-20
b. With Perseverance	James 5:7-12
c. With faith	James 2:14-26

7. Confession
a. Forgiveness	1 John 2:9, 10
b. You get what you say	Mark 11:22-24
c. Bind and loose	Matthew 18:18, 19
d. Accountable	Matthew 12:36, 37

III. How you receive power
1. Power belongs to God	Psalms 62:11
2. You shall receive power	Acts 1:8
3. Intercession	Colossians 4:12, 13
4. Power is within you	Ephesians 3:20

IV. Rules of prayer
   a. Jesus taught us that prayer must be accomplished by faith (Matthew 21:21, 22)
   b. He taught that prayer must be offered in His name (John 16:23)
   c. He taught us to pray simply (Matthew 6:7)
   d. He taught us to pray in secret (Matthew 6:6)
   e. He taught us to pray persistently (Luke 11:5-8)

     f. He taught us to pray with humility (Luke 18:9-14)
     g. He taught us that we need to be right with others when we pray (Matthew 6:14, 15)
     h. Praying the word of God preserves our life (Psalms 119:25)
        *NOTE: We must cultivate the art of turning a promise into petition and instruction into intercession.

V. Receiving Prayer

1.	Dwell and abide	Psalms 91:1
2.	Be quiet	Psalms 107:28-30
3.	Be still and know	Psalms 46:10
4.	Listen for a still small voice	1 King 19:11, 12
5.	Know when to keep silent	Ecclesiastes 3:7
6.	Caleb quieted the people	Numbers 13:30-32
7.	Be thirsty	Psalms 143:6

VI. Model Prayer

1.	Who you are praying to	Our Father who art in heaven
2.	Praise (God's name)	Hollowed be thy name
3.	God's authority & power	Your kingdom come
4.	Your agreement with God's will	Your will be done
5.	Where God's will is done	On earth as it is in heaven
6.	God is our provider	Give us this day our daily bread
7.	God's forgiveness	And forgive us our debts

8. We must forgive	As we forgive our debtors
9. Speak to the situation	And do not lead us into temptation
10. Ask God for help	But deliver us from evil
11. Praise God	For yours is the kingdom and the
12. Amen = I agree	Power and glory, amen

VII. Prayer delays
 1. The Bible teaches that answers to prayers might be delayed for various reasons, but these delays are not denials (Daniel 10:10-13)
 2. Mary and Martha waited extra days for Jesus to act on their request (John 11:6)
 3. Moses prayed to enter the promise land, but he had to wait fifteen years for an answer (Deuteronomy 3:23-29)
    - NOTE: Prayers in accordance with God's will and for His glory are always answered. Prayers alien to the mind of Christ and His purpose don't make the cut. Effective prayer is found in a right relationship with God.

VIII. Prayer goes unanswered
 1. When it is substituted for necessary action (Exodus 14:15, Joshua 7:7-15 & Ephesians 3:20)
 2. When it seeks to change God's declared decrees (Deuteronomy 3:23-27)
 3. When it ascends from an unclean heart (Psalms 66:18 & Laminations 3:8; 40-44)

4. When it seeks to advert deserved and necessary chastisement (2 Corinthians 12:7-9)
5. When it totally disregards the known will of God (1 Samuel 8:9, 10)
6. When it is offered in arrogance and foolish pride (Proverbs 8:13)
7. When it is prompted by selfish ulterior motives (Matthew 6:5)
8. When it arises out of a heart full of ill will and hatred toward others (Matthew 5:24)
9. When it simply expresses meaningless and repetitious phrases (Matthew 6:7)
10. When it lacks sincerity and faith (Matthew 6:5, 7 & Hebrews 11:6)
11. When it is inspired by carnal motives and not by the Holy Spirit (James 4:2, 3)
12. When it is unaccompanied by confessed conscious sin (1 John 1:8-10)
13. When it seeks the recall of lost opportunities (Luke 13:25-28)
14. When you are in strife (James 3:16)

IX. Specific Prayer Needs

Specific prayer needs	James 5:13, 14
Fellowship with the Father	Matthew 6
Asking for help	Luke 11
Spiritual warfare	John 17 & 2 Cor. 10:4, 5
Generational curses	Daniel 9
Boldness	Acts 4
Praying for nations	1 Timothy 2:1-4
Every good gift	James 1:13
Travailing	Galatians 4:19

Mental & spiritual prayers	1 Corinthians 14:14, 15
Tongues	Romans 8:26, 27
Continual prayer	James 5:16
Consecration & dedication	Luke 22:42
Faith	Mark 11:24
Ministering to the Lord	Acts 13:2
Worries	1 Peter 5:7
Commitment	Psalms 37:5
United prayer	Acts 4:23-30
Wisdom	Colossians 1:9
Love	Philippians 1:9
Spiritual blessing	Ephesians 1:3
Attitude toward prayer	Romans 1:9-12
Revelation of God's knowledge	Ephesians 1:16-23
Deliverance	2 Chronicles 20:6-13
The mystery of Christ	Colossians 4:3
Church	1 Thessalonians 3:11-13

X. Praying in Tongues
  1. Praying in tongues builds up your faith and keeps you in God's love (Jude 1:20, 21)
  2. Praying in tongues gives thanks to God (Colossians 2:6, 7 & 1 Corinthians 14:17)
  3. Tongues helps you to think like an adult (1 Corinthians 14:20, 21)
  4. Speaking in tongues gives you rest (Isaiah 28:10-12)
  5. Tongues speak to God and edifies you (1 Corinthians 14:2, 4)
  6. You know all things through the Holy Spirit (1 John 2:20, 27)

7. Revelation knowledge comes through tongues (1 Corinthians 2:6-13)
8. We have the mind of Christ (1 Corinthians 2:16)
9. Renews knowledge (Colossians 3:10)
10. Praying in tongues is praying in the spirit (1 Corinthians 14:14)
11. Tongues can be interpreted (1 Corinthians 14:13)

XI. Praise

1. Praise is warfare	Psalms 8:2
2. Clapping	Ps 47:1,5
3. Shouting	Isaiah 42:13
4. Playing musical instruments	Isaiah 30:32
5. Dancing	Malachi 4:2, 3
6. Singing	Isaiah 35:10
7. Whistling	Judges 5:16

Prayer for Salvation

Father, thank you for loving us so much that you sacrificed your son for the whole world's sins. I believe that Jesus bore my sins on the cross, died and was resurrected from the dead. Please forgive me, and help me to move away from self-centeredness toward Christ-centeredness. I invite Jesus to come into my heart and be my Lord, to rule and reign in my heart from this day forward. I lay down my life, and I believe that my old man died with you on the cross. I put on the new man, and I ask that you send me your Holy Spirit to help me obey you, and do your will the rest of my life. I fully expect to see changes in my life for the better as I read your word, fellowship with you in prayer and obey. Thank you for forgiving me. In Jesus name I pray, amen.

Calling Prayers:

1. Father of love,
I believe you are my encouragement and strength. Thank you for giving me your best in Christ. Thank you for your calling upon my life. I know that you have called me to greatness, and I accept and agree with your call for my life. Give me insight to the full nature of my calling that I may run my race well. Father, you are greater than any circumstances that would interfere with what you have called me to do. I thank you for you prepare the way before me and let me know what to do and say and pray in every situation. Thank you father for you know the beginning from the end, and you direct my steps with great confidence. I take comfort in this knowledge and rest in your abilities and wait on you to bring about the necessary changes in me to fulfill your calling upon my life. In the mighty name of Jesus. Amen!

2. Father, great is your love and great is your name. Your amazing love has helped us to be your children. As one of your children, I ask for your favor this day. I ask, "That I may know the length, the width, the height, and the depth of your love." Father, help me to understand mysteries and speak wisdom that will edify brothers and sisters in the faith. Help me to shine and to move when you say move and speak what you tell me to say. Daddy Father, you are my help. You are my hope. You are my all and all. Thank you for answering me quickly and giving me supernatural results to my prayer. In Jesus mighty name, amen!

Called

3. Lord, great is your mercy. Thank you for your mercy. Have mercy on _____ and me and show us your love. Let us dwell in your love. Let us be taught by your grace. Let us make wise choices based on what your grace has taught us. Thank you, father for peace in my heart and soul. Thank you for teaching me to rest in you. Father, I love you. Thank you for today. Thank you for the favor you placed on my life. Thank you for what you have accomplished in my life. You are my hope Lord Jesus. You are my peace. You lead me into rest. Thank you for success. Thank you for forgiving me and helping me to be forgiving. In Jesus name, amen.

4. Father,
I pray for _____ & _____.
Help them to see you and know you and be known by you. May they know the length, the width, the height, and the depth of your love. Keep them from the evil one, and lead them not into temptation. Warn them when they are in danger and when they are around dangerous people. Give them wisdom in every situation that they face, keep them in health, and prosper them. May angels guard them and watch over them. Let your word stick to their hearts, be watered, and produce the mighty crop of salvation. In Jesus Christ's name, amen!

5. Father,
The love that you have for Jesus dwells inside of me. You have helped me grow in Christ. You have given me love that can not be taken away by any means. You have shown yourself strong on my behalf many times. Father, I believe the love you have for me is more real than any situation that I'm about to face. I ask that you

hold my hand and lead me through this next phase of my life; that I'm walking with you step by step. Father, give me warning that I may pray for a better outcome, and indeed realize better days than I have in my past. Holy Father, Christ Jesus our Lord and conquering King, it's my greatest desire to see you in all your glory when you come to destroy the rulers of this age. Let me see great things. Let me be your end-time warrior. Help me to prepare for these blessings and help me to see immediate financial success and extremely great health. Father, I know that you have already given me these things, but I am asking that you show the world that your signature is on the ministry that you have already called me to and have given me to do. Thank you, Father for your love and support. Amen!

6. Father, Christ Jesus our Lord,
Great is your name. Thank you for the gift(s) you are giving me. Thank you for fore knowledge and preparing me to receive what you are giving me. Thank you, Holy Father, for your purposes being fulfilled in my life. Thank you, for giving me the desires of my heart. Thank you, for hope and for giving me a vision of the victory to come. Maranatha! Come Lord Jesus! Come quickly! Amen!

7. Father,
Grant me the strength to hold onto your word and not let it go until it achieves it's purpose in the lives of those I'm praying for. Let me know when I'm in danger and around dangerous people. Help me to know when to do something that needs to be done and let me know when something needs to be left alone. Give me wisdom beyond my years and alert me when someone needs prayer and/ or help. Give me the wisdom to do

what needs to be done. Thank you, Father for helping me everyday. In Jesus Christ's name I pray, amen!

8. Father,
Thank you for directing me in my daily life. Thank you for the spirit of truth that guides me into all truth. Lord, I ask that you save me from myself. I realize that I can be selfish at times and desire things that are harmful to me. I believe that you love me and you are helping me to be Christ-centered. Thank you for helping me and giving me what I need to move away from thinking, words and actions that are not only harmful to me but cause me to loose effectiveness as a witness. Thank you, Father for your direction and guidance. In Christ name, amen.

9. Lord,
Thank You for giving me the desires of my heart. Thank you, for placing your desires in my heart. I ask that you wake me up to what is going on around me. Help me to walk circumspectly. Father, help me to know without a doubt that I'm helped by almighty God. Destroy unbelief in my life and help me to give no place to unbelief and doubt. It's my greatest desire to submit unto you and resist the devil, so there is victory in every area of my life. Thank you for your grace that teaches me and your love that passes all knowledge. In the name of my Lord and savior, Jesus Christ, I pray. Amen!

10. Father, thank you for helping me to be where I need to be at all times. Thank you Father for you help me to see beyond the physical. Father, I pray for a deeper relationship with you. I want to go further and further into the depths of your love. Help me Father to be free from Satan's lies. Deliver me from his annoying voice.

Father, thank you for peace in my heart and helping me to enter into your rest. Thank you, Father for helping me to know you more. In Jesus mighty name. Amen!

CALLED WORKOUT

James Bible Study
    James is a book of wisdom that shows you how you can move toward or away from God-centeredness. It's a great place to start hearing the call of God on your life.

1st Day: v1:1-4
Faith tested = Perseverance: this leads to perfection.
How can you preserver in your present situation?

_____
_____
_____
_____
_____
_____

2nd Day: v1:5
Ask for wisdom
God gives wisdom to all who ask regardless of your faults.
Does all include you?

What do you need God's wisdom for today?

___

3rd Day: v1:6-11
Don't doubt! Doubting has consequences: leads to not receiving from God.
V9-10: focus:
If you are poor, focus on the positive.
If you are rich, focus on humility.
Do you have doubt about something God has told you?
Are you unsure about something?
Review v5 and pray for wisdom.

___

4th Day: v1:12-14
Being tempted: The root is self-centeredness
What is tempting you today?
Review v5 and pray for wisdom.

5th Day: v1:15-16
The process of falling away from the faith.
Where are you in this process?
Review v5 and pray for wisdom.

_____
_____
_____
_____
_____
_____

6th Day: v1:17-20
God-centeredness
Root yourself in these words.
What questions come to mind?
Review v5 and pray for wisdom.

_____
_____
_____
_____
_____
_____

7th Day: V1:21-25
Planting the word in your soul is a process of hearing and doing.
Reflect on what you've learned so far and put it into action.
Review v5 and pray for wisdom.

_____
_____
_____

8th Day: V1:26-27
Watch what you say
Pure religion is helping the helpless.
When you catch yourself saying negative and hurtful things, stop and repent.
How can you help someone today?

9th Day: 2:1-13
Treat everybody the same.
Think about how you treat others richer and poorer than yourself?
Do you treat anyone different than others?
What should you do different?
Review v1:5 and pray for wisdom.

10th Day: V2:14-26
Faith without works is dead.
What are you believing for today?
How can you work your faith to receive what you are believing for?
Review v1:5 and pray for wisdom.

_____
_____
_____
_____
_____
_____

11th Day: v3:1
Teachers receive heavier judgments.
Why do you think teachers receive heavier judgments?

_____
_____
_____
_____
_____
_____

12th Day: v3:2-13
Life and death are both produced by what you say. Therefore, watch what you say.
Who are you in Christ?
Start confessing who you are in Christ today.

_____
_____
_____
_____
_____
_____

13th Day: V3:14-18
Strife vs. Peace is the same as
Self-centeredness vs. God-centeredness
Romans 8:1-14
Examine yourself!
Where do you see yourself in these verses?
Ask God for His plan for peace in your life.

_____
_____
_____
_____
_____
_____

14th Day: v4:1-6
Self-centeredness
Examine yourself! Are you friends with the world?
Pray

_____
_____
_____
_____
_____
_____

15th Day: v4:7-10
God-centeredness
Root yourself in these words
What comes to mind?
Pray

_____
_____

Called

16th Day: v4:11-12
Don't speak out against your brother:
1st go to him personally
(Mat 18:15-17) & (1Tim 5:19)

17th Day: v4:13-17
Don't make your own plans. Follow God's plan and will for your life.
John 10:1-4
Reflect on your future plans.
Are these plans your plans or God's plans?
Pray

18th Day: v5:1-6
self-centeredness. (Mat. 6:24 & Lu 16:13)
Is your focus on money or God?
Pray

_____
_____
_____
_____
_____

19th: v5:7-12
God-centeredness
Are you like the farmer preparing for the harvest?
Are you grumbling?
Are you enduring?
Are you doing what you say you'll do?
V5:12: see Titus 2:11-14
Pray for wisdom.

_____
_____
_____
_____
_____

20th Day: v5:13-18
Prayer
Are you praying for others?
Are your prayers getting Elijah results?
Are you confessing your trespasses?

_____
_____
_____
_____
_____
_____

21st Day: 19-20
Watch out for each other and help those who are falling away.
Ask the Lord to help you to be sensitive to the needs of others around you.

_____
_____
_____
_____
_____
_____

REFLECTION

Look over the 21 day workout and reflect on your progress.

1. What did you learn?
2. How did you apply what you learned?
3. Pray for wisdom
4. What did you hear?
5. How can you apply what you heard?

_____
_____
_____
_____
_____
_____
_____
_____
_____
_____
_____
_____
_____
_____
_____
_____
_____
_____
_____
_____

Called

Additional thoughts or comments:

Called

Contact Information

IMmanuel Magazine

www.IMMagazine.org

E-Mail: Called2begreat@Gmail.com

CPSIA information can be obtained at www.ICGtesting.com
260256BV00001B/4/P

9 781612 158334